Dedicated to

MARY BETH, ALEXIS

and all the others

Do not stand at my grave and weep;
I am not there. I do not sleep.
I am a thousand winds that blow.
I am the diamond glints on snow.
I am the sunlight on ripened grain.
I am the gentle autumn's rain.
When you awaken in the morning's hush,
I am the swift uplifting rush
Of quiet birds in circled flight.
I am the soft stars that shine at night.
Do not stand at my grave and cry;
I am not there. I did not die.

Anonymous

A NEW AGE HANDBOOK
FOR
DEATH AND DYING

by

Carol W. Parrish-Harra

Devorss & Company
P.O. Box 550
Marina del Rey, California 90291

ISBN: 0–87516–470–6
Library of Congress Card Catalog Number: 81–70369

Printed in the United States of America
by Book Graphics, California

The author wants to acknowledge the many who helped. First of all, Charles, Bethany and Jared who believed I could do one thing more. Then appreciation to Eileen, Laura, Sharon and Lois who spent hours typing and proofing. And thanks to those who read and encouraged, and especially to those whose lives became our material.

CONTENTS

Foreword

Whilst I have read this book, my chief feeling is the wish that there were many more people like the author! It is written with such a rare, tender and thorough perception of all that human beings go through, that it is bound to be a comfort and inspiration which is much needed in the world today.

This period in history is producing such intensive suffering, bereavement, homelessness and unemployment all over the world, that only the most inspired, fundamental and vigorous help will be of any consequence. The author of this book has an esoteric and psychic background, which enables her to write from experience. One even feels that she could, if she would, say much more regarding the hidden causes behind the apparently unreasonable sufferings which are the lot of many who do not seem to merit them in any way. But she realizes with great wisdom, the value of being *natural,* of weeping at need, of accepting personal comfort from others, as well as giving it; and of avoiding, above all, the danger of repression with its long aftermaths.

One finds some of the phraseology very beautiful, and other parts expressed with abrupt common sense. There is something for everyone in this encyclopaedia of dying. Christ spoke about our "second birth." One feels that he referred to the birth of the soul *within* the body, when the human aspiration makes it possible. This book deals with the "third birth," when the individual, having passed through the essential *school* of physical life, is re-born, plus acquired maturity, into the expansive wonder of the inner worlds—surely a moment of intense rejoicing?

Vera Stanley Alder
Bournemouth, England

Introduction

Each death is a poignant love story. Each drama is unique and special, just as each birth. We dare not avoid these powerful experiences because DEATH IS LIFE TOO.

In the past five years I have been sharing with a few people some stories of great value to me. These stories are real. They are dynamic in their implications to me and to my picture of life. This book is my personal conversation with you about them.

A part of my ministry is devoted to assisting people to heal and to hope, even in the face of death. Paramount to this is the belief that just as there is a natural time to be born, there is a correct time for us to die; a proper moment to let go of life as we know it and to begin anew at some other stage.

Established ideas of heaven and hell are familiar, and fortunately, in recent years, significant research has seemed to reinforce the idea of continuity of life. Old ideas are being presented in the context of newly researched experiences of those who have been resuscitated and revived, and a fresh picture is coming into focus. A new vista is opening that will facilitate better understanding of spiritual teachings, inspired writing and sacred script concerned with death, giving help and hope to many who are not yet certain about what to believe.

I have experienced many kinds of death in life—the death of hopes, prejudices and relationships, as well as physical deaths of loved ones. But my near-death experience when I was in my twenties totally assured me there is more to life than we readily acknowledge. Later experiences reconfirmed this.

As a counselor, I use the material in this book to prepare persons for their own death experience. You will find proposed methods to encourage open expression of fear and unrestrained questioning so that some comfort can enter into life at this delicate and special time. In addition, I make suggestions for the construction of a precious and close-knit support system for each participant during the final period of time. This unity is most beneficial for the survivors as well as the one passing. All points expressed in this book have been raised during actual experiences and have proven valid in helping to expand limited and painful views of death. I believe you will find in these insights comfort and a greater assurance of a living Creator with a perfect plan.

Carol W. Parrish-Harra

A NEW AGE HANDBOOK
FOR DEATH AND DYING

CHAPTER ONE

Dare We Ask?

Much of our horror of death
comes from the feeling (even though it
may never be expressed) that it is the enemy of
life. We love life; therefore it
is natural to dread death. But death is
no more the enemy of life than sleep is
the enemy of work and play. Sleep
makes it possible for us to work and
play the next day. Death makes it
possible for us to live on. It has
therefore a real contribution to make
to life in the large, being the gateway
through which we slip from the lower
life into the higher, from the briefer
into that which is eternal.
—From *The Bridge Is Love*

Death is a common denominator of life. Each of us faces the experience as one who hopes or one who knows. Those who don't know, suffer. The purpose of my sharing is to ease that pain. Whether it be for one's self or for the loss of a loved one, I wish to offer my own very real experience in order to give comfort.

The mental and emotional suffering surrounding death is most often the result of fear of the ultimate unknown. In

1

each of our lives, there have been fears we have either acknowledged as realistic or have explored and found to be unjustified. The healthiest response to fear is action, either fleeing the object of fear or turning to face it and hopefully to break its hold. Since there is no escape from death for any of us, the wisest course is to learn all that can be known of it, to diminish that which is unknown to nothing, if possible.

What is known of the experience of death? In the last decade, researchers have explored many aspects of that process. Emotional stages leading to the acceptance of one's own death or the death of a loved one have been examined. Perhaps most startling of all has been the finding that hundreds of people resuscitated from a physical death —people who would have died without medical intervention —experienced very similar series of events. What did these experiences have in common? Death is most often comfort, freedom, and relief. All those who remember these experiences try to give this comfort to others.

Raymond Moody, a medical doctor and former college philosophy instructor, has written two books, *Life After Life* and *Reflections on Life After Life,* based on his study of individuals experiencing apparent bodily death and then returning to life. His work, published in 1976 and 1977, offers us experience after experience to ponder. As we read, we discover those little known, personal experiences that have always helped humanity in its search. Dr. Moody, now intending to become a psychiatrist, really wasn't trying to prove life after life, but sought to collect experiences for study. He analytically reviews, arranges, and presents material in as scientific a way as possible, allowing the reader to draw personal conclusions.

Spiritual thinkers all tell us with confidence of the continuation of life. Their own experiences of recall, conscious death or near-death experience, or spiritual mysticism have given them a sureness. Most of us need to hear of these shared experiences to encourage us as we tiptoe to the edge of the abyss and look into the face of the unknown.

Why is death unknown? First, because its veil is so thick, we can no longer embrace those who enter its portals. Next, we have no framework in which to place stories of visions of returned loved ones and of their comforting touches. If we're educated, intelligent, or disciplined against wishful thinking, what are we to do?

What we are to do is to look at death with new eyes. Cycles of life and death are everywhere about us teaching us the magic formula: plant the seed, wait for growth, full-flowering, energy receding, then death. Trees do it; so do marriages, mortgages, school years, and businesses. We call the shorter cycles by other names, but did not your death as a child allow the adult to emerge?

Look at how long man has been learning to die daily by surrendering himself to sleep, turning off an awareness to the outer life to live within. Could this be practice for death itself?

Will you remember with me the greatest loss you have ever felt, even though it may have been the most painful experience of your life? Was it the death of a dream, a hope, or a person? Try to allow yourself to feel the loss now. Do you remember how something inside took hold and you began to change? Whether you wanted it or not, change occurred.

This is the law of the universal life force . . . change and grow, or die. The flower blooms its great glory and then the blossom dies. Are we not life's flowers and have we not given our best blooms accordingly?

When the change to death threatens us, a great deal of the trauma comes from falling so completely out of control of our daily lives. We have a need to feel a degree of control, although certainly, at times that degree changes. For years we've envisioned what we were going to do. We have built plans, hopes, and dreams. We've pictured those we love with us all the way and cannot see life happy and meeting our needs without them. Now, with this change of events, we've had all this taken from us and we know of no tool to help us regain control of the situation . . . no way to stabilize our lives and restore our pictures. Of course, one part of our logic knew these things could happen, but we had not woven it into our plans of life. Now, some mysterious force has taken over, or entered into our experience, and as always we have problems with our unacquaintance as well as our helplessness.

Death symbolizes the ultimate loneliness . . . the end, and as a symbol, it is without all . . . without life, love, knowledge, friends, without body. We are alone . . . ultimate loneliness . . . and if this be so, how can we stand it? Death also does not allow us to avoid it . . . now we are helpless. Death has the power and what are we to do?

The simple answer is in seeing that in our daily living we have had only partial control anyway. To get us started, it helps to find the philosophical answers, the belief, or the courage to go on one day at a time; to keep on keeping on.

Most people equate death with separation and loneliness, at least subconsciously, and herein lies the trauma. With new ideas, philosophical concepts, and scientific studies, we are finding this is not so. Reading of the beauty in the hundreds of collected stories from persons who have died and revived sheds light in great abundance on this previously hidden experience. Yes, there is the separation from one level to another and it surely is rough, but so can life be rough on this side of the veil, and very often is rough as death approaches. I believe this difficult time helps us to let go from both sides. It may be an important key, especially for those of us remaining behind. The new awareness of love, tenderness, guidance and caring that is shown from the spirit side brings comfort to the one transferring residence, as well as the ones left behind.

Our aim is to learn to live and experience without fear of

life or death. It is in this ideal state that we can be fully developed, expressing our potential. Fear restricts, holds back, limits our ability to give and receive, and whether it be fear of life or fear of death, it works against our fulfillment of Self.

The root of this fear of death is the lack of knowledge about it. As consciously awake life participants, we know, we live, we think, we anticipate. And it's terrifying to think about not knowing or not planning, or even worse, not hoping.

There are many who tell us that the experiences of inner life are as vast and varied as those of outer life and we can't know about this inner life unless we live there. Is that believable? Why not? Reality is personal and unique. I don't know about everything that exists in outer life, do you?

Life and death are flip sides of the same coin. I think of a shoreline. Where does the water end and where does the beach begin? When are we asleep and when are we awake? Are we asleep while dreaming, or living in an inner consciousness?

If we can begin to expand our definitions, we will realize the cycle of life and death within. Medical thought offers us the idea of cells constantly being replaced. Bacteria live and die within our form. We are always throwing off dead cells and tissues, but notice that we do not see this as death. It causes us no pain. Sleep, the death of this day, is natural because we live in firm belief of awakening tomorrow. We do not fear sleep; on the contrary, we often welcome it for the rest and restoration it brings.

Think of the satisfied feeling of a busy, pleasant day in which much is accomplished: the happy-tired of a job well done. Can we approach our final sleep with the same happy-tired?

The country was traumatized last year by a gentleman who chose to die naturally by declining to eat. His grandson recorded the entire process in poignant photographs. When they were published, screams were heard of cruelty, neglect, and sadism! Were we not to look at this process? Did we wish to deny a man's right to finish living in his own style?

Another elderly man, my precious friend for about ten years, went to bed one night and died in his sleep. All alone in his own home, in his own bed, he made the change from outer life to inner life. Many are concerned about living alone, but this man was not. He had chosen to be alone and one day his living was done. He just finished living. He didn't die of anything; he got through living. He had finished the experience on this side of the coin.

When the natural cycle of pregnancy is completed, we call one born; when the natural cycle of physical existence is completed, we call one dead. Wouldn't it help if we think of dying as another birth . . . into a spirit life? And in this birthing process, shouldn't we expect spirit help? Of course . . . and I shall share my knowledge of this assistance with you in a later chapter.

What is the objective of a study of death and dying and exploration of life after life? I believe facing the facts of life and death fully allows us to deal with our fears, guilts and shame in a direct and meaningful way so we can live more freely now and die more freely when it is the time.

CHAPTER TWO

Can Death Be Birth?

Throughout the years of my ministry I have been with a number of persons when they were approaching their final moments of life. Each experience has added a piece to the puzzle for me until I've seen it is time to pass on what I've learned so that for others, some of the pain may be avoided. My experiences with life after life do not stand alone. Mystical Christianity supports and reinforces this study. Lecturing for spiritual study groups and for the human potential movement has made me aware of the large number of persons who have had a "beyond belief" encounter of seeing something that others didn't. But who dare they tell? As I share and encourage, I hope others will find the way.

My earliest memory of a perception of which others were unaware was as a child trying to explain to my grandmother that I was seeing "smoke" come out of a pet duck I had received at Easter. She assured me that there was no smoke in a duck. Shortly thereafter, she saw the duck dead, and she knew I had indeed seen "something." I knew then as a child that there was more going on around us than most people could see.

I have met death as a friend and so have others I have been with as they were making their transitions. In a perfect way, the pattern seems to be much the same. Always, as the hour of death approaches, angelic beings, more beautiful than you can imagine, join the one-in-process. Because I have observed this pattern for so many years, I look for three radiant, angelic types of beings. Most everyone is aware you can feel death, as we say, in the air. There is a feeling of other-worldliness; you might say the vibrations change. At the time of the end, or near the time of the soul's withdrawal, the being at the head usually moves to the feet and directs the process. If someone is physically present and at the feet, he will invariably shift to one side when the being moves into this space.

The two beings on either side gently rock the body of the one passing. I believe this gentle rocking action lulls and comforts and also serves the practical purpose of separating spirit and matter. The aura can be seen around a person until there is less than six hours before the transition. You'll get some time variation according to the youthful vitality of the physical body or the intensity of the soul within. Then, the energy connection between the physical, emotional and mental faculties are dulled and the light gradually goes out.

A peace flows into the room and into the person who is passing. The spirit body or soul, when freed, rises and follows the spirit at the foot of the bed as if unaware of anything else. For a time, the relief of being free seems to be of the most importance.

Later in this book we'll review Dr. Kenneth Ring's work in which he examines these patterns more closely. Dr. Ring is a psychology professor at the University of Connecticut and has been researching these last moments of life. My experience has convinced me that these moments are relief-giving for the individual passing and for the survivors. I respect the importance of this time as an overlapping of dimensions and I think everyone participating and present can feel the distinct difference in the quality of these moments.

My perception helps me compare the deathbed process to the childbirth process, with the angels of death serving as midwives to help the spiritual being make its re-entry into the non-physical world. Just as we see a baby helpless and ill-prepared for its landing here, needing some special assistance, I have seen the beings of the spirit world come to assist in the reverse process.

Religious traditions speak of angels, spirit life, visions of saints and visits from those in the spiritual dimension. But what about those who are not quite sure about such "mythical" traditions? Those who espouse any religion have to examine their ideas or faith in a new light when the death experience nears for them or someone they love. The major message of Christianity is eternal life. The celebration of Easter, as a principal church holiday, is to underline the message of Jesus' personal resurrection and the promise he demonstrated, so all can believe in life everlasting.

Prior to the Christian era, the idea of a next stage of life existed. Some sects of Judaism taught that at the coming of the Messiah all would arise, even those in the grave. Within the mystical Kabbalistic teachings it is said there are always souls seeking bodies in which to return.

The Hindu tradition, in its most ancient and its most present form, teaches that life manifests on several planes and that the physical world is a place for experiencing. In a non-physical state, one rests. Then, one experiences birth and life again in the physical world for further learning or growth. This cycling is called reincarnation and few westerners truly understand it, much less realize that three quarters of the world population accept the concept and that the early Christian Church, the ancient Greeks, Romans, Egyptians, Pythagorians, and Hebrews respected the idea.

As the West evolved into a materialistic age and such things couldn't be examined in a scientific laboratory, less and less respect was held for spiritual, non-physical theory. And the Christians, following the trend of the times, dropped the idea.

A beautiful comment was made by the famous church-man, Dr. Leslie D. Weatherhead, when asked if Christians could believe in reincarnation. He answered, "Can Christians dance? Some can and some can't."

Today, many individuals feel reincarnation is provable; others feel it is not. Scientifically approached, an excellent piece of work has been done by Dr. Ian Stevenson of the University of Virginia, entitled, *Twenty Cases Suggestive of Reincarnation.* Most libraries have this volume if you'd like to explore further.

This, my friends, is the sum of it. When someone accepts reincarnation, it is logical as well as comforting. More and more are inclined to review scriptures to see if, in fact, there is in the Bible a basis for the belief.

Whether or not one accepts reincarnation, I want us to deal here with the idea of life continuing in *some* form, one with which we are not yet familiar.

In the Bible, Jesus tells us little about heaven, but often makes it clear that some dimension other than this world does exist; and he repeatedly states that there is eternal life. Certainly this idea deserves much thought. Jesus' teachings, vital to Christians, seem to parallel the words, "Then the Lord said to Moses: 'You will sleep with your fathers, and will rise . . .'" The Bhagavad Gita, the Hindu scriptures, teaches: "That which is non-existent can never come into being, and that which is can never cease to be." As a theory, eternal life seems to be everywhere, but is it really believed?

It is not unusual for mystics, philosophers, or spiritual students who have developed strong inner lives to remember previous existences. At a point of stillness, generally in meditation, the contact is made and a flash or segment of another time is revealed.

In addition, the public has developed such an interest in hypnotism, many have recalled past life experiences, in-cluding deaths of many types. When talking with these individuals, they recall vivid details. Remembering sometimes causes discomfort until the hypnotist suggests they will observe rather than feel the death. Next it is suggested they describe what they see as they watch what happened to their bodies, and some will tell of moving to the spirit world in words very like those of Dr. Moody's subjects who had near-death experiences.

This raises many questions, of course, and jars the traditional views we may have. I believe that most of us who have these experiences fight hard to put them into our traditional religious experience for as long as we can. I know that I certainly wanted to feel in step with my church and had no idea of separating myself as insights and visions began to occur. In time, one either accepts the inner direction as one's truth and reality, or rejects it and believes one is at best, very peculiar. Great help came to me when at last I became acquainted with philosophies which spoke of other lifetimes and the writings of mystics and sages that told of their priceless experiences.

Albert Einstein said, "Scientists will turn their laboratories over to the search for God." I believe we are certainly seeing such as this occurring now.

Humanity gradually accepts new ideas and throws out the old. Each age of sophistication complicates the matter. The primitive awareness that was spirit-based in the minds of simpler cultures was displaced; we replaced it with the power of logic and material achievement. As we focus our attention more and more on this physical aspect of materialism, we are losing the awareness of the non-physical. The many mystical stories of saints become accepted as the fantasies of a fervent, adoring heart rather than the experience of an expanded mind. The obvious relief or bountiful joy at the bedside of one who is dying when he says, "Can you see him?" or, "My mother is here" is always welcome. It is rarely understood, but for all who are present, it is very real. No words of examination are raised at this time.

Only later does the mind ask its questions, and many

curious minds are asking them in our time: "Does consciousness continue? Is there a next stage of life?" Scientists, doctors, ministers and the general public all clamor for an answer. Indeed, all minds are challenged. Some now know and no longer ask. Certainly, at the present time, we need to entertain exploration.

If I am dying (and I am, as we all are), I wish to ask the questions, examine the answers and find peace. If I were planning a trip to Europe, I'd go through much the same process. From the moment of birth, we move through our cycle of life; for some brief, for some lengthy. If we wake up to the Game of Life, we can learn to win at the game.

To play the game successfully, I have to move ahead from where I am at any one point in time. To do that, I have to let go of something: the single life to become married; freedom to become a parent; job security to become an entrepreneur. The letting go takes courage. Damn, does life ever take courage! Every step. Letting my children go takes more courage than I can muster at times, and yet, it is destructive to them and to me if I don't.

What is it about being trapped between a rock and a hard place? It's life, with its demanding process of change. Going forward or backward, but lo and behold, we're going!

The ultimate change in physical life is death. As we go toward and through this process, even it has variation, alteration, and stages.

CHAPTER THREE

Each Snowflake Is Unique

Just as the author of a book must keep in mind the purpose of his effort, a major requisite in any counseling done within the death and dying framework is to be aware of one's goal. As I see it, the purpose is two-fold. First, one must meet the emotional needs of the person who invites one into the experience. Second, one should aid each person in constructing a theoretical framework that will give comfort and support as the death experience occurs.

What goals these are! How can one proceed? My experience has taught me that most well-meaning friends and counselors tend to get the cart before the horse. Generally, they intellectualize the situation and give lots of theory, rather than taking the simple initial step: Begin by just caring. Then, with great respect, allow your loved one to have his steps and stages in his own style and stand by fully loving and supporting. Appreciate the uniqueness of his character and help without judgment. This is unconditional love in its fullest.

What do I mean by style in relation to the dying process? Let me share examples. A gentleman, who fully accepted the role of a good, family provider, moved to Florida from a northern state. He and his wife had spent the winters in the south for several years. He was dying slowly from progressive advanced cancer, and planned ahead all details: to move his wife, dispose of northern property, get a new, choice model, mobile home, teach her to drive, get paper work done, etc. It was an approximate two-year program, carefully constructed to make sure his wife would be secure. Thus, his style was to do everything that was physically possible, and he did it. Unfortunately, he included little conversation about himself and his wife, their children, their life together. When we got into counseling, he needed help with the expression of love and the repair of his inter-personal relationships.

Another example, a terminally ill woman I visited a number of times, asked me to help her because she and her husband had never had a conversation about her death. She shed tears as she told me, "I love my husband and want to say some things to him and every time I try to get started, he says, 'Now don't talk that way. You're going to get well and next summer we'll travel.'" My task in support of her was to broach the subject of death to the husband and push the ball into action. I had to be the "bad guy" and get it out in the open.

One day at the hospital, when I purposely arrived during his daily visit, he said he'd wait in the lounge until I left, but I insisted he join us. As he made small talk, I said in a soft voice, "You know she is dying." He jumped to his feet, exclaiming, "How can you say such a thing? Especially right here in front of Thelma. We're getting the best care. If you can't be cheerful and help her, you shouldn't come here!" He had to come to her defense. He thought he was protecting her from pain. I gently continued by saying, "She knows she's dying and she needs to talk about it with you. If you are the one with whom she has shared so much of her life, her companion and best friend, she needs to be able to share her fear now. That's what I'm trying to get started."

At this point it was my responsibility to comfort both of them for a few minutes so she could gather her ideas together and he could adjust to the unthinkable thought of such a sharing. Now I could speak of unfinished business, touching, living one day at a time, until it would become a matter of one hour at a time.

When I left, they were talking in a new way. In a few days he came to see me to have a private chat, and I continued to see her for the next few weeks. They grew close; she had the support she needed, and he began to grieve, letting down his barriers, and they shared intimately the last weeks. I am certain he made better progress in adjusting afterwards because he really had shared the dying experience with his loved one.

Only once have I really gotten into a forceful, dynamic battle with a patient over facing realities. An incredibly strong lady, she was a counselor herself, and also a student of mine. Her life had been difficult and she had managed to hold herself together through a divorce and other major disappointments. She was bitter and very mental. She embraced metaphysical thinking and believed she could will anything into being. This woman was ill for a time; changed her diet, did meditations, studied much, and seemed to improve. After a series of tests, she told me there was no longer any sign of cancer. A year or so passed; the cancer reappeared and progressed rapidly. With vigor, she began her exercises of meditations developed by Dr. Carl Simonton at his clinic in Texas.[1] She affirmed perfect health and had some very meaningful dream and meditation experiences as she embarked on a mission of willing herself to health.

I know many people who have achieved great things using the techniques my friend engaged in. There are many programs, each working for various people in various ways. I encourage people to try these processes, for I believe we are responsible for our own health.

However, in this situation, there was no improvement.

1. Simonton, Carl and Stephanie, *Getting Well Again.*

She kept her spirits high and at a point, she called me long distance and asked that I come.

As I arrived, my friend was sitting upright in bed, emaciated. She couldn't have weighed more than fifty pounds. Normally of small build, at this point she was merely skeletal. I saw her breathing through an oxygen tube and having lost her hair long ago, the sunlight gave her the appearance of a fragile, young child. She announced she was ready to be healed and wanted me to pray for her. She was sure of her will to live and positive that she could rid her body of the enemy. So beautifully valiant and determined a woman, she was convinced her method should be to use her will against the will of this intruder.

I tried to talk to her about her condition before we prayed, but she wasn't to be sidetracked. Finally I said, "Have you faced the fact that you might not get well?" She exploded in anger. How dare I open the door to doubt! I was her friend. How could I suggest such a thing?

She spit out angry words. I began suggesting that healing has many meanings. It certainly means wholeness, a well-being of all the parts of the person. For example, a physically well body doesn't always constitute perfect health at the mental or emotional levels. We sharply discussed forgiving, loving, letting go of the anger. She acknowledged the anger as the major force that had helped her go through all of this; that she was going to beat this like she'd beaten many other obstacles. I made another suggestion: Healing could mean peace, well-being, and having right action in her life. It could mean it was to come through death; therefore, death could be welcomed. We finally prayed together for love, peace, and the releasing of all that was destructive for both of us. I truly prayed for guidance, and after more conversation, I left.

I walked away knowing I had kicked down her false game. She was only fighting herself, only using the same tools she had used in her material life to play the game. I was sad I had been so direct, but I had felt so impelled. It had seemed so important that some of that "false upper lip" be done away with. She had needed to forgive. I knew I wouldn't get back for some time; the next day I left for Texas for six days, promising I'd call as soon as I returned.

Later, when I telephoned, a considerate lady answered: My friend had died. It was done. My heart was heavy. I had wanted to be tender with her, and thought that perhaps I should not have met her forcefulness in such a challenging way. I called a mutual acquaintance immediately. She said, "Carol, do you know about our friend?" I answered that I did, and she said, "You helped so much; she cried a lot and later called me and talked. She was different for three days, soft and happy. Then, two hours before she died, she called the ambulance and asked them to come and get her, she wanted to go to the hospital." A great weight fell off my shoulders. If the technique had helped, it had been valid. I needed personally to know that it was. Never had I met such a demanding, strong-willed person, and I had come on equally strong to help her. I had doubted. Now I understand she was being true to herself and I was being the same, and because she knew I cared for her, she listened. She went to the next stage of life with real peace. I wept tears of thanksgiving.

I hope these examples say, "Don't expect dying individuals to be alike, no more so than we are alike in any other expression." Surely the first step. is to avoid laying our belief system on dying persons; express concern, but talk about the topics their other support people can't; and show, through unique ways, that we're not afraid to be real with them at this time. It is also important to avoid thinking because we are well, we are in charge of the game. As I see it, part of the difficulty support persons have had to deal with is that they are unfamiliar with the dying and death process and they need to become acquainted with the do's and don'ts.

No expression of caring is as potent as touching. Do touch. Some things you can say with a touch you can't say with a word. As long as it doesn't produce pain, I believe one should stroke, massage, rub the feet, massage the arms and hands, or just plain hold hands or lay your hands on their bed or body. Due to the sexual orientation in our lives, we tend to stop responding with this openness and deprive each other of such comfort. It's time to come back to a rich appreciation of what touch can do.

Understand, however, that theories and ideas about counseling don't help very much until we have nursed our own emotional nature. We need to demonstrate our ability to care, to listen to the outpourings, to support another person in some way. If we and they connect in the love area, if we can create an emotional trust, then our opinions and realities may be helpful. The typical thing that occurs is that professional and prepared people try to explain their perspectives to the dying or the support persons from a detached, intellectual level. My experience has proved to me that no matter how valid these points are, the mind is not what's hurting . . . the emotional level is in pain; death and parting are great emotional pains. We must acknowledge this to ourselves. I have no qualms about tears coming into my eyes or holding someone and crying together. I'm not suggesting I become unsettled, but I certainly do feel deeply and caringly, and I do allow myself to respond. My eyes often fill with tears. My heart is filled with admiration for the courage, love, sacrifice and goodness that I see every day in human lives.

I find it a sacred place into which I am admitted. Being truthful and saying simply, "If I can help, I'd like to," I offer ideas. These ideas are gifts, free to be accepted or rejected. I believe people need to talk through feelings and thoughts, most certainly to talk through fears. Some do not need outsiders; many others do. Some can read an article or a book and get inspiration.

Dying should be as much a part of the life as eating, birthing, sexuality and business. Dying is living, too. If I have to hide it something is unnatural. I should be able to find my way in this as in any other endeavor. Those who are sharing my life should share my death as well. Otherwise, we both miss an important part of the whole.

CHAPTER FOUR

Moving Through the Stages

The beautiful work of Dr. Elisabeth Kübler-Ross defines the five stages of death. They are (1) Denial; (2) Anger; (3) Bargaining; (4) Preparatory Depression; and (5) Acceptance. Each of us passes through these stages and according to our personality and experience, the stages last longer or shorter or hold more potency for us. I have a friend going through a period of separation from her husband and she is going through these stages. The "death" we deal with does not have to be the death of the physical body. Whenever life presents us its great drama, we, too, go through these stages and adapt to them in ways that suit our unique life styles and characters.

Dr. Kübler-Ross' work is definitive about the cycles of one's experiences in the dying process. It is clear that all are dealt with, but not necessarily in a set order. I agree with her, because in the years I have worked in this area, I see these patterns consistently repeated.

(1) Denial

Dr. Herman Feifel, M.D., author of *The Meaning of Death*, shows great insight when he says we don't really feel our mortality until we lose our parents. So very true; in our youthfulness, death is usually way out there. Yes, we know we will experience it some day and, intellectually, we accept the idea. When we lose our surviving parent, we stand stripped of a front line; we are next . . . and most of us move on, still avoiding the issue. Unconsciously our society denies its mortality by being overly involved with youth: dressing ten or twenty years younger, acting 25 at 40, erasing years through cosmetic surgery, needing an affair to show we still have sex appeal. We delegate sickness to the doctors and the patient care to the nurses and the hospital. Even if they are close friends, we hesitate to visit those who are terminally ill, not because we don't care, for we truly do, but we don't know how to act, how to cry, or how to face this event. We shun speaking about meeting death. Because our society believes doctors and nurses should know how to do something about this alarming condition, we're angry when they can't. We say quickly, "Get another doctor," or "He doesn't know anything." When a patient dies, the doctor is considered to have failed. We feel he didn't do enough to prevent it. Consequently, doctors have been programmed to withdraw emotional support from the patient, simply prescribing whatever it takes to keep one comfortable.

There are plenty of stories of hard, uncaring nurses, so used to death they bitterly follow hospital rules. Today, many nurses are among the first to recognize there is a need for a new approach. They realize they get burnt out from their emotionally exposed role and many are asked the questions: How? Why? What? These health care personnel are probably the closest to the problem of denial.

Many times they act out their own denial in their relationships with patients, or interact very little to avoid getting into a soul-searching conversation which they feel inadequate to lead. I think we can all be helped by realizing the patient leads that conversation. We are doing our best by just listening and caring, encouraging the flow, and gratefully accepting the opportunity to think along with the patient.

The dying patient dealing with denial is exactly like ourselves at other points of denial in our lives. Remember losing a wallet, or your child doing some incredulous something that your head couldn't accept? This denial is the same feeling. Our system keeps spilling out the information that, "These things happen to other people, not to us!"

After a period of gradual restructuring of our day-to-day reality, we find ourselves able to handle the idea of death. Of course, variations of this stage exist; particularly if you have been suspecting the problem before it was confirmed. Many times one goes from test to test or doctor to doctor and this is helpful to the restructuring of our reality. Hard as it is, it's a necessary part of being able to get past denial.

Sometimes one is unwilling to face the imminence of death and chooses not to reveal it to others, pretending for a while that it isn't so. I've seen great acts of sacrificial love come about this way, for some persons cope better by not acknowledging the truth of their mortality until some internal goal is reached. But the process is working within the person. I think when denial is this strong, anger and bargaining are burned up in its furnace. Later, when the acknowledgment finally is made, the patient is moved successfully toward acceptance.

While the dying person is engaged in this denial stage, it may be possible to effect healing by a shift in his consciousness. Such a healing requires openness to the soul level, or openness to the phenomena sought through meditation . . . coming into contact with the Divine within. Spiritual healing is the term used, and commonly a person with strong spiritual energy will assist in the healing. The goal is to ignite the lagging, natural, healing power of the patient. If the patient can achieve this change, touch in to the cause and the building anger and release it, healing may occur. If the shift occurs past this point, the physical pattern is generally set and deterioration is usually too far along.

(2) Anger

As I counsel, I am constantly reminded that life energy becomes restricted and renders us less effective when we are filled with fear, hate and anger. These are the major enemies of life. Fear paralyzes, hate kills and anger consumes. When we are fearful, we say, "frozen with fear" or "frozen stiff." This is exactly what happens. We stand still, can't think and do not feel. We can't love or care or deal with the day-to-day experiences.

Hate kills our loving nature. Just as the love-warmth within us naturally gives off vibrancy and comfort, hating restricts our precious, vibrant spirit and destroys those about us. The hating flows outward like a poisoned stream, a disturbing negation moving against the life force of others. It kills or cancels out the vitality of life force it encounters. Spiritual students are taught to make their lives a blessing. They are to radiate their goodness, vibrant nature and compassion outward, to serve as a channel of enrichment to be shared.

Anger is the strength trapped and turned inward. It is the fury of the storm suppressed. Anger eats away at our personality until the substructure caves in. The strong body weakens, the fire breaks through in burning words of destruction, or the hostility consumes our relationships. Anger burns like a volcano, out of sight, until one day it erupts and cascades into view. A spectacular event and certain relief, but painful and weakening for those in its path.

A woman I worked with last year admitted her anger at God for taking her husband. Theirs had been a good marriage, twenty-nine years long, and he had been a real companion. Her natural reaction was, "Why him, God? Why not a couple who fights, a couple wanting to be free of each other? Why him, when I need him so?" These are the hard questions asked so frequently. There is no acceptable answer. The reality is that through this experience, both parties took a step forward to begin new stages of development.

This lady, by crying out her anger and thus freeing herself from it, found the way to do for others what she had needed done for herself. She decided to be the kindness she wanted others to be. She knew she had hoped for gentle words and patience, so she spoke gently to others and was patient with them. If life wouldn't be fair, at least she would be! Working through her anger, she took a giant step forward. The spare love, hidden away with no mate to receive it, became compassion to be given to those who touched her daily life.

Death isn't God's love or lack of love, it's the pattern of life. We will learn that life is just as valuable as we realize or perceive it to be. What is it about time, that one day can seem so long that it is agony and another day can rush by so quickly that we hardly savor its flavor? There is this same relativity about a life. The more we become aware, the more wisely we learn to use each day and each opportunity.

(3) Bargaining

As anger is released, a person usually reaches the time to face and experience a period which is called bargaining. It seems to me that it is in this stage that many patients reach out for some kind of help. As a minister I get a large number of calls at this point.

As the shock and anger are burning out in a patient, the pains of parting, the recognition of unrealized goals, and the dread of death become agony. The burning fear of never holding a beloved one again makes itself felt and we are not yet ready to face that. Suddenly we feel the poignant pull of those future things we were going to do. We don't know how to face death and we recoil from the thought.

The fear of death registers within our nature; it jolts us to such a degree we now savor the life we had been taking for granted. Day-to-day experiences take on a new poignancy and the bittersweet days begin. . . .

There is now a readiness to bargain. The patient will start

to pick up the pieces and either live a spiritual life, find he can endure surgery, stay on a strange diet, try fads or reach eagerly for whatever anyone suggests. "I'll do this, this and this, if in return someone, somehow, can make me well." Many people begin to bargain with God through prayer, particularly intercessory prayer: "I'll do anything, Lord, just don't let this happen to me or mine." They are grasping, searching for something to help them hope. We need to realize that through this agonizing time, many do find hope and answers and some find life extension. It is important to realize that this process of bargaining is most natural and very productive.

Intercessory and memorized prayer becomes sincere and deeply honest. The response is one of reaching for the awareness of something more, greater, stronger, and as the days pass, the empty chaff is burned away. The real richness of life is seen for the treasure it truly brings.

As prayers go out, change comes day by day. Interestingly, the change comes most frequently from the purifying experience of prayer itself, not any remarkable or miraculous outer event. The bargaining stage lasts until the approaching death becomes an undeniable reality.

Some persons, well ready for death, have a shorter struggle at this stage. Others bargain longer, seeing death as defeat, failure or an alternative beyond the realm of possibility. Some, by their philosophical nature, are already living one day at a time and these latter usually pass through this stage with flying colors.

The hardest hurt while bargaining are those who put too much hope in each cure sought out. It matters little if it be the latest nutrition fad or a spiritual healer. It is similarly hard for those who have no hope. Hope is the elixir of life. Without it there is no light to shine on present beauty. Those without daily hope allow themselves no growth, no joy, no betterment. So, seek to encourage the idea of improvement and the possibility of the goodness of life, if not the extension of that life. The key now is new appreciation of each remaining experience rather than more of whatever life is.

Personally, I do not believe anyone can answer all the questions that are asked in this reaching-out phase. I think it is necessary for the struggle to be met. The questions need to be asked. The feeling of questioning must be wrestled with. God must be challenged. I relate to this as the necessary meeting of force with force. Bargaining, questioning, struggling cause change within both the patient and the survivor. God is no longer the one who has sentenced us to a cruel fate but now becomes a Sustaining Presence. Gradually we feel secure knowing there is a potent pattern to our nature just as we feel security in the pattern of morning following night or one season following another.

Obviously, not everyone needs to make his peace with God. Some certainly do—but remember to allow the uniqueness of each one to have space. Here is a special place and time for remembering that a rose must be a rose and geraniums will be geraniums. The "old crab" will go cranky to the end. Why not? We dilute life to one color if we allow only one style in which to die, just as it would be rather dull to have only one way in which to live.

So let's adopt a code for ourselves. Let's allow the perimeters for experience to be broad enough to include the differences in personality as we all go toward our final experience. Let's think in terms of uniqueness, not good or bad, or right or wrong. Let's try for gentleness, patience and openness. Some days we'll make it; some we won't. We will do the best we're capable of each day!

Remember, "What the caterpillar calls the end of the world, the Master calls a butterfly."[2]

---

2. Richard Bach, *Illusions: The Adventures of a Reluctant Messiah*

CHAPTER FIVE

To the Destination We Come

We've come a long way by the time we have finished denial, anger and bargaining. In some ways the great emotional swings are behind, yet we have one more mighty battle ahead. In her work, Dr. Kübler-Ross[3] tried to graph these stages for us; we can see where we've traveled and what lies ahead (see p. 28).

(4) Preparatory Depression

This next stage of dying usually becomes apparent after bargaining is gradually left behind. Now, we feel powerless; we are in that place of "What's the use, anyway." Generally what is happening is that we are recognizing it is just a matter of time until death, and often the picture that is painted seems too painful, too disfiguring, too much of an effort to face. Discouraged, tired of struggling, usually uncomfortable, we need some time to make inner adjustments.

Where is our fighting spirit or our positive outlook? Can we maintain our fine image of ourselves? Do we want to, or is it worth the try? For what? Life sure hasn't lived up to our expectations. We're just getting started . . . if it had only been a year or so farther down the line. If only . . . but it's now.

Dr. Kübler-Ross calls this stage, preparatory depression, the lowest point on the journey. Here it seems one goes

3. Elisabeth Kübler-Ross, *Death, The Final Stage of Growth*

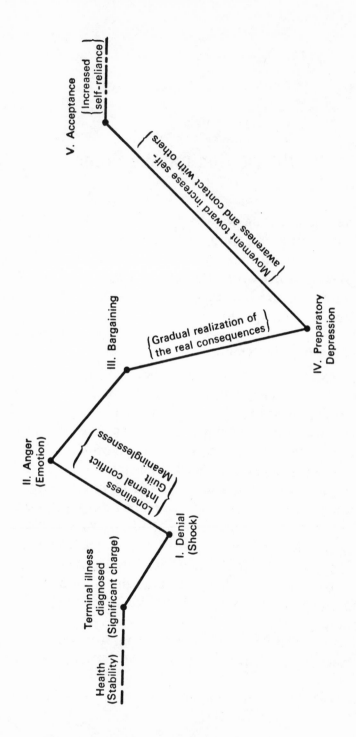

Graph reproduced by permission of Dr. Kübler-Ross.

inward, breaks contact to a great degree with those who love and care, and spends at least a time in a kind of personal mourning. I believe it's important that we allow this part of the process and do not try to deny the reality of it. I use the word mourning here because I think it's the death of dreams, hopes, future plans, etc. Even as in final physical death, I see this same withdrawal from relationships at the time of divorce or at the loss of children. This mourning period is for the death of little self and its private treasure of unplanted seeds. It is only after this stage that the more aware human being can come out for the last experiences of the life. Preparatory depression is a great movement forward to increase personal awareness and after it is found, one reestablishes contact with others.

My attempts to counsel families, to encourage openness, to bring death into the center of the circle are to ease this particular part of the transition process. It is best not to avoid but to guide the experience while the dying one makes his own inner effort. The family and close ones need much help at this stage. Maybe we who wish to be supportive make our greatest contribution at this point. Here again, individuals are very special and the pattern differs from one to another.

(5) Acceptance

One of the recurring marvels of life is the manner in which the death of winter gives way to the reborn life of the spring. From time immemorial, thoughtful men and women have mused upon this wondrous rebirth of nature in the spring season. They can see in it the deep meaning of the restriction and struggle and the rebirth and exaltation of human life.

Let us liken this cycle to the reaction that occurs when one struggles with his dying ego. Tired of bargaining and losing, he prepares for the next step of life or death.

After the struggle, one can move to acceptance, rebirth, a period of increased self-reliance. The body isn't doing so well, but the spirit is getting better. It senses a new adventure and rises to meet the occasion. The courage awakens; now the strength, new-born and beautiful, can flow outward and the family can feel love moving again.

The dying one, at this stage, most often awakens admiration in others. Within the hearts of those who watch, occasionally there is a wish for it to be over and they question, "How much longer can this go on?" At the same time, there is a kind of growing awe at the strength of life, for it has been thought of as fragile and failing. If the loved one is heavily medicated, this stage is often missed. If he is aware and awakened, the insights and perceptions of what life is all about are awesome.

The brave soldier facing death, ready to go into battle and knowing what is to be faced, is tender but strong. He consciously looks deep into our eyes, knows us for what we are and encourages us to face life with equal courage.

In the preparatory depression stage, the dying one's attention is focused inward to examine and re-evaluate. Now, in the acceptance period, as the attention is again focused outward, he or she can sincerely care about those left behind. There is freer and more open conversation, a wiser self-sharing in the planning, unless, by our signs, we signal "Don't say that, I can't stand it," or some other denial signal that says, "Stop, I cannot go with you on this part of the journey."

I think it's wrong to reject our dying one at this stage of his coping with death. Right here, as the wisdom and character of our friend is most achieved, we signal him to close off. We, in our pain, deny him his chance to speak. At the evaluation of a life's living, ready to flow, we say, "I don't want to hear it—say something else, pretend, protect me, play my game." I want to yell to these people, "Be still. Sit down and shut up!" I would turn to a dying person in this stage and say, "WISE ONE, what do you see? Tell us what life has given you."

If we can have ears to hear, the beloved shares the words we'll be treasuring in a future time. The wisdom and comfort come, the advice, the words may be tough or tender, but here is the bloom of the plant, the evaluation of what that person has gleaned. There is some unfinished business, of course, and the wisdom now comes for it to be completed. The one who needed our comfort a short time ago can now comfort us.

With the patient's renewed strength, courage and willpower to help us, many previously non-shareable experiences can be explored, discussed, forgiven and released. As the patient has broken through to the hidden reservoir of inner strength, now we are lifted also. The pain is not so great any more. Most of the time the unbearable is bearable and we live more freely. Feelings are understood more readily, symbolic expression is very meaningful and communication is much more satisfying and requires less effort. Rarely is self-pity apparent at this point in dying; most are courageous, especially if death has been discussed and everyone is prepared.

This time lived well inspires and sustains the survivors at a future time. To remember the direct and honest eyes of our loved one when he has worked through it all and has shared with us, even if in bits and pieces, helps us to know life is of great value. For the last "I love you," for the final touches of personality, we stay close by as the fire of his life smoulders, giving its last warmth to us. We see the change from physical strength to the shadow body as our loved one is molded for the next stage. We give to him, he gives to us, comfort, love, and togetherness. We send him on his way bountifully surrounded with our love.

If only dying could always be this ideal. More and more, with new tenderness on the part of helpers, and new methods by the professionals, death is becoming understood. At times the acceptance process does not seem to be lived well; it is tough, lingering, and unconscious. Don't be fooled by the physical wrapping, for the acceptance of death is happening out of sight. Support the dying one. Touch more lovingly; increase your expressiveness. Allow this one you care about to find his style.

Here's our chance to love and understand. Our loved one has his way of being, which isn't going to change. Remember, this stage will be made in the image of his powerful personality! If he habitually looks out for others, that will show. If he is used to taking charge, he'll busy himself telling you what to do in the time ahead. If he tends to be quiet or picky, it'll show, but behind this is a new strength and awareness that what is his to do is really his. Self-reliance allows him to direct you, knowing he does not seek your assistance. He is in charge of his days. Enjoy that part. Rejoice in the strength he has found.

In this clarification of the dying process, a key for the support people is to observe the stages calmly, not to rush or push to make things happen in a specific pattern. Understand the five stages as colors of a rainbow. They will all be there, overlapping and touching, not always in the identical pattern, but all contributing to the total effect.

It is meaningful to understand that the insights to be gained from this process also may be deeply helpful to the survivors and to those who were support persons and who must now go through their own five stages in releasing a meaningful tie of friendship and love.

When I lost a premature infant and was critically ill myself, my grief moved quickly through the five stages. My self-survival mechanism kicked in and, although the experience was painful, my thankfulness at getting well, surviving to return home to my other children, became important. The getting well became the focus point and the life healed more easily. At a later time, when a second son died at childbirth and I was not critically ill myself, the loss was much greater. The personality centered itself more on the loss than on the surviving process and the agony persisted.

When we lose a loved one, we begin a process of looking back prior to the death. We replay our experiences with him. Using the memory for comfort, we often try to change reality to get relief. I believe this is most natural. However, sometimes one gets stuck in the past and cannot shift back and forth. He now becomes ill. Remembering happy moments with the loved one is needed to give us positive energy for today to help us realize how good life really is, and also to give us courage to greet the next new stage of our personal life—indeed, to inspire us to seek this stage's hidden treasure.

Our ability to adjust is the law of survival. All of us learn that we survive many things we think we can't and many things we didn't even want to. It's amazing how much the human spirit does survive.

Think of the unnatural pain created by concentration camps, kidnappings, rapes; the traumas of being wiped out by fires, getting lost in storms, airplane crashes, wars and injuries . . . the list is endless. And many times the victims fare better than their families. The recovery of the victim is focused upon and that one often finds his way back to reasonable life and functioning, stronger than before. But near him, feeling the pain but not focusing upon himself, is the parent, mate, or other close one. The survivor has gallant spirit and reveals it. The others often experience bitterness, or paranoia, or turn inward.

No one can focus on death and dying and not find life and living more precious. No one facing death consciously —and we are all facing the change—can avoid the realization of how much we yet need or want to do. If you have a year to live, make a list of your goals; afterward, make a list of what you would do if you knew you had only two weeks left. Do these things. We should all be living up-to-date. Have a major goal for achievement. We need to be doing the most important thing each day of our lives! This way we do not let unfinished business remain unfinished.

CHAPTER SIX

Sudden Death vs. the Expected

To those whom death has left desolate let us call attention to the words of the great teacher, Sri Krishna:

"Thou Grievest where no grief should be!
Thou speakest words lacking wisdom! for the wise in heart
Mourn not for those that live, nor those that die.
Nor I, nor thou, nor any one of these,
Ever was not, nor ever will not be,
For ever and for ever afterwards.
All, that doth live, lives always!

Never the spirit was born; the spirit shall cease to be never;
Never was time it was not; end and beginning are dreams.
Birthless and deathless and changeless remaineth
   the spirit forever.
Death hath not touched it at all, dead though the house of it
   seems!"

—Sir Edwin Arnold

It has been established that those who are dying must work through various stages in the death process; those who are surviving have equal emotion with which to deal.

Most of us have some very guilty feelings after a death. We remember the person with our heart aching and always wish we had said or done one more thing. This is most certainly true of a sudden death.

We have another conflict with which to deal as we face a

34

loss, and that is our own feelings about what is best for ourselves versus what is best for the dying person. We experience great feelings of guilt if we want dying to hurry and get over with; equally so, if we feel we just can't let someone go. If we hold to the thought that we can't live without him and our loved one lingers miserably, we feel selfish; if we want it over with, we doubt our love for him. Both leave us feeling guilty.

We need time to adjust and release, to work through our conflicting emotions and, even though one part of us is grieved to see the end occur, there is another part which is glad it's over. The period of illness helps us here. If there is a long illness, or old age, we have a time for sorting out, expressing concern, doing some extra thinking. At least we are partially prepared.

The sudden, swift-moving death blow is by far the hardest for most to handle. We aren't ready. We are left up in the air in the midst of life. We have so many nagging after-thoughts, wishes, and desires now never to be spoken. Our minds can recognize that the sudden death experience may certainly keep our loved one from the suffering which we really didn't want. But we feel the relationship ruptured within us, and rarely can this heal as naturally or as quickly as in the lingering illness process.

Always there is dispute comparing the sudden death versus a long, lasting illness. Truly, neither is better than the other. Each has its own particular struggle and its own type of compensation.

When one is dealing with the awful, painful, day-to-day suffering of a loved one, sudden death seems so much easier. But we must remember, with a sudden death, there is no last lingering touch, no planning together, no seeking advice and working out of family matters, no visits from family and friends. There is no gradual adjustment and releasing that is natural as you watch a body change, abilities fade, suffering deplete the life force.

True, the sudden death seems merciful to the victim, but would he not have desired one day to put things in order? And doesn't every survivor think about this? A planned, last encounter would mean so much. A last kiss, a tender touch, a forgiving conversation could save years of regret and inner turmoil.

When we are dealing with sudden death, we have more to think through alone. We have to forgive and release. From within ourselves we have to make well that which has occurred without the interaction of the one that has gone. The process depends so much upon our own self and usually we are confused and hurt and can't function really well. We seem to go in circles repeating over and over, last words, last actions, the story of the occurrence. We seem to be trying to make it acceptable to our own mind. I think of it as trying to untangle a large knot. The knot is our hopes, our dreams, and our plans for the future that became scrambled with the death event.

I remember, as a child swinging high in the air, a sudden slip and then the jolting sensation of hitting the ground. Shocked, stunned, with the air knocked out of me, I remember the feeling of trying to reorient myself. This is not unlike the feeling of sudden loss. Your picture of family, friends, your personal reality are jolted by the blow and trauma of unexpected death. The blank feeling of non-reality sweeps in and out. The emphasis centers around catching one's breath just as from the fall from the swing. The head spits out the situation with "This does not compute!" It is now that the basic self-discipline, consideration and concern for others, endurance and freedom of expression that are deeply ingrained in each personality can serve us. Those traits we call character, deep and underlying our personal approach to life, are revealed. The mind kicks in and out . . . sometimes sharp and alert, supplying all the data we need, sometimes failing us completely. Names won't come; memory fails; our logic refuses to function.

As the computer spits and sputters, trying to get caught up with the events of the moment, the basic qualities of personality express.

There is no right or wrong way to cope. Society has constructed some guidelines so each of us, individually, will not have to re-think what to do. Too many guidelines block natural expression so we have come now to reject many of them that formerly served the purpose.

Today we are quicker to demand our way! We want to be free to be our unique selves. As a people, we seek honesty rather than the pretense of drama. We are desirous of being free to be. The right or wrong way to deal with any death situation depends upon personal need, character, style, ethnic background. To sum it up, it depends upon each of us—our custom and our need.

For everyone, it is important that we deal with the experience in such a way that healing may occur in our lives. Our system innately knows how to heal and adjust. It has done so many times in several different turns of events. Our inner strength can soar; we can heal and hope and live once again. How we handle the experience of pain and loss either moves us toward healing or blocks the ability to rebuild and repair.

When the stunning blow of sudden death strikes, there is a period of functioning at reduced capacity. However, I have observed in many, the ability to function well, to plan; realization flows smoothly for a time, then suddenly, one can't add two figures or remember what time it is, even though one has just looked at the clock. For these people it is easier to function for the first day or two than it is a week later. When the immediate crisis demands decision, it is absorbing and one can rise to the occasion. Later one will find the mind cutting in and out. This is the natural, mental adjustment that has to happen to integrate the occurrence.

We usually adjust our picture of life a little at a time.

Our views gradually change direction like a plant bending and growing toward the sun. We move the plant; again it reaches for the sun. Gradual change comes when we approach life one day at a time. Sudden death is like transplanting a plant to new soil in a new setting. The new, different reality throws the system into shock and our grasp of it all must occur gradually.

When one is in a state of shock, the mind doesn't accept impressions readily. At this time, so much of ourself functions on rote that facts do not register in the usual way. Forgotten details, misplaced items, getting confused is the rule, not the exception. It is as if the many abilities contract to a slower rate that we may survive. Gradually, as the inner adjustments occur, the ability to bounce many balls will return. It is important that we do not condemn ourselves or feel poorly about these mishandlings, but rather know them to be a part of the process. It is a natural part of our survival mechanism and, in fact, our future mental and emotional health depends on this process. While trying to absorb events and adjust to change, it is perfectly natural for persons to tell the same happening over and over; or for families to re-run past events, to question, repeat, and struggle with the same points again and again. While to an outsider it may seem unnecessary, important inner adjustments are occurring and those who wish to be supportive and helpful have to understand the great value of this catharsis.

Be aware that we have the same process of blankness with shock as we have in great happiness or pleasant surprise. Remember the stunned look on the face of someone caught unaware at a birthday party or shower. Remember the awesomeness while trying to comprehend the beauty and majesty of the birth of a first child as the parents study the miniature form for hours, amazed at their part in creation. This integration process of all change takes time as new vistas open within one's self. It usually takes years to put experiences into true perspective and to see growth and change. For the survivor, I think the goal is to deal honestly and well with whatever comes.

How can we deal with the guilt of unfinished business? In the sudden death we are miserable until we either anesthetize our feeling self or move through our grieving cycle.

Somewhere we have gotten the idea that being hurt, emotional, or upset at a loss means we're not a good sport or we are weak. Because tradition has strict rules about how to deal with death, we follow the rules . . . receiving words of condolence, planning a proper funeral and burial, and accepting helpful acts from family and friends. Because we follow tradition, in return we are supposed to receive relief!

It doesn't work. It just plain doesn't happen. So we freeze up and act as if it did. Frightened at the prospect of not being able to cope, we clamp down on ourselves and become numbed, walking, talking zombies. If anyone comes upon us crying or upset, we pretend it's all right, saying, "I'm sorry I broke down," or some other polite remark, pretending we're not coming unglued. "I know I should be over this," or, "I don't know why I'm crying," are repeated to every friend, counselor, and minister. I often want to shout to the world, "It's okay to grieve! Scream! Cry!" We need to thrash it out so the loving being inside can come to life again. We must unlock that knot in the stomach and the tension held in the mind before the love and natural creative thinking can flow once again.

Stifled emotions haunt the carrier. This is not to say that everyone must scream. One will scream, cuss, and shout. Another will sob softly, "Why?" Many get busy, shifting into the activities that must be accomplished. Some need to sit quietly and review the entire tie, as if talking through it sorts out the pieces and lets them be filed for safe-keeping. Each of us must have time to finish this business in a way that is natural.

Can these natural emotions be emptied out or guided to the surface in some positive way? If we are to be aided by the releasing of these enemies of life, how can we do it? Aren't we too afraid of it all to empty out? My own feelings in these kinds of circumstances have made me aware of the dread of letting go for fear I'll never get hold again.

As a counselor, many times I have led someone on that fine line of emptying out in order to renew life . . . to let go of the dead bird in the hand to reach for hope and truth in the bush. Is this not death and rebirth again defined?

CHAPTER SEVEN

Confronting Pain and Grief

A father of a beautiful young girl, who had died unexpectedly as a result of a short, swift illness, could not get well and return to living until she appeared to him in a deep, meaningful dream and kissed him and said, "Daddy, I love you." With this love, life began again in a heart grieving and closing. She came to comfort and to heal his pain by her presence. Again and again those beings living in their next stage of life make us aware of them. Do we readily speak of this to our neighbors, or even our families?

How hard it is to say, "My reality is different from another's." How often we keep our secret; stifle our words so we do not give ourselves away. Many numbers of people have said to me privately, "I need to tell you, so-and-so appeared to me and said, 'You'll be all right,' or 'I love you.'"

If death has abruptly ended a meaningful tie, the pain of unfinished business has to be worked through. Several things can help. First, our spiritual belief that life continues may help us talk to that being and release our feelings. Second, especially for an active individual, it helps to do something the loved one would have liked or respected, in his memory. I do not necessarily mean a "name plaque" approach, but some volunteer work, more time with the children, a new creative endeavor, taking care of oneself, or any activity that gets one involved with releasing the guilt. Families usually find that each member wishes he had done something more and they often need to share their feelings in such a way that each helps the others trigger underlying emotions.

I recently spoke to a lady who is employed and away from home each working day. Two years ago her husband died suddenly after a brief time of retirement. One of her major regrets centers on not going home from her job to fix lunch for him. Truly, it would have been a difficult task to accomplish; logically, she never knew her lunch hour from day to day, and the distance, traffic, and rush ruled it out. Now, she is really hurting and feeling guilty because he made his own lunch.

Essentially, the guilt is a cover-up for much more. Guilt masks our present fears as well as holding us to the past: We didn't realize . . . we believe we could have done differently . . . we wish we had been kinder, more thoughtful, or even home more often. These thoughts are saying, "I didn't express enough appreciation of life then, now I am pained about it." They are also saying, "I'm not being as good or as useful now as I can be." If our up-to-date life is full and the actions of today satisfy us, we release guilt. The only antidote for guilt is action; an action which incorporates the value of our past experience and puts it into use today.

Yet, always the close survivor feels some guilt as the result of a loss. The mate that continues to live feels pain acutely and questions, "Why him or her, instead of me?" This guilt effect is even more pronounced in a sudden death situation. The shock of the impact, plus having no time for "unfinished business," magnifies the guilt. When an accident occurs and one or two persons lose their lives, the survivors believe they should have done something differently. If an accident takes four or five lives, great guilt is suffered by any survivor. If one is an automobile driver, the first one out of a burning building, or one who survives lightning which strikes a group, repeatedly this one has feelings of guilt. It isn't logical. Most of our feelings regarding death are not logical. They are emotional in nature and when attempting to be a support person, we must first do the comforting from that level. After the emotional pain has died down to some degree, we can give some philosophical and intellectual comfort. Rarely is a survivor ready for this in the very first stages of grief.

True enough, the spiritual and philosophical undergirding of our lives is our great, built-in strength. But do not expect these strengths to prevent or protect us from the searing pain of loss. They will help us later, in due time. The awareness of already integrated comforts and our established beliefs do sustain us, but the waves of pain are from our emotional level and are not to be denied. A dangerous fallacy is to think that our faith has failed us as we realize our pain and vulnerability. Harmful remarks are often made by well-meaning friends when they suggest, "I know your Christian ideas will comfort you now." "As strong as your faith is, I know you'll be all right." "Your beliefs will not fail you, you're a good_____."

We will doubt our faith if we compare ideology and pain. Faith is structure; pain is pain. Our pain isn't lessened by faith. Our comprehension of the change is helped by our belief system. Be careful in making faith remarks. Only if we are very close and of the same ideology should this even be considered. It is much wiser for support persons to realize the tenderness they touch when entering into spiritual or philosophical areas. Touching, loving remarks and sincerity are much more powerful tools to help. When the emotional nature is in great pain, administer the balm there. At another stage, the intellectual level will be ready for questions and answers—the unanswerable "why's," the damnable "if only's." Then, and only then, will spiritual and philosophical answers help. The rule I try to remember is to respond to the level most in need at the time. When there is something to do physically, do it: touch, help, expedite plans, clean, cook. When the waves of pain are searing our loved one, respond emotionally: comfort, shed tears, express affection. It's the only language really understood. When the mind is in agony, questioning and struggling, use rational ideas and philosophical concepts. Talk from personal beliefs and share how your ideas serve you. Help a person with his query. Support him while he builds or grows a philosophy or rethinks his ideas. Express your continued support on as many levels as you can comfortably do so, but adjust your focus to the signals the survivor gives. Remember this simple formula: Physical need requires responding physically, emotional need requires responding emotionally, and mental need requires responding mentally. It often takes a bit of time to get the formula working, but it is invaluable as a tool.

A beautiful practical nurse once told me in conversation that she had looked death in the face so many times, it is now an old friend. I have thought about this remark many times and I would note that as we encounter death again and again, we begin to see it as natural and we get over our fear. It is human to fear the unknown. As long as death is kept from being part of life, it will remain the dreadful unknown. As an integration occurs, death is seen as the natural close of a life just as a sunset is the natural conclusion of a day.

My grandfather was paralyzed for several years as I grew up. I played and scrambled about him. He told me stories and visited with me a lot. I do believe he was one of the greatest influences I had in my formative years. The fact that he was restricted to home gave me companionship and someone I could always talk to. I don't remember being particularly sad about his paralysis. My feeling was more, "that's just the way it was." Today I like to remember that after his death, for our last goodbyes, we brought his body home and set the coffin in the living room where his hospital bed had been. I think his life and death have helped me in my work with others.

Death is healing, too, in its natural sequence. Death ends the life experience, lets one out of a body weak or used and helps that soul to go about its business of being. When the body fails to respond to therapies there are reasons. First, the individual has a block or trauma in his system that isn't able to release, at least at this time, and there needs to be work done. Second, the body's answer is no. The healing force is helpful, but well-being isn't returning. If life is threatened, we must realize that death may be the natural sequence for this situation and individual. Whether we like it or not, death brings healing and release through new life of a different sort. Knowing this profoundly helps us, even though death is not our choice.

A way we might look at the death of a relationship is by comparing it to trimming back a branch of a plant. The branch is cut off abruptly, but around that ending starts new growth. When death comes into a life, much the same happens. An outlet closes and new growth sprouts. Habits change, new interests must spark, friendships awaken and adjust, we put out new sprouts into which life energy may flow.

If we do not start new growth as a plant does, we begin to restrict our own life energy. The plant loses its vitality and like it, we too begin to die. For a time after repotting or trimming, a plant hangs in there, neither living nor dying. We know we should see new signs of growth quickly or the plant will not make it. So it is with us: When the shock, the trauma is released, our focus must shift back to constructive life and new growth. We allow our memories, our love, and our experience to give us new compassion and an expanded comprehension of life going on in and about us. I would like to share a technique that has been important to me as I repot and trim in my own life each year. I write a lengthy, up-to-date letter to each of my children at New Year's. To me it's my "this-is-where-I-am-with-you" review. I need to bring everything into order so I have no unsaid, unfinished business. I like the feeling of being current with these loved beings, asking nothing of them except to receive my outpouring. It helps me to let them know that I care.

The whole experience of life, as I see it, is made up of gems and jewels of drama which say, "I care." Touching, poetry, birthing, tenderly feeding and romancing, all are saying, "I care." We are loving creatures. Our natural nature is to care. Loss interrupts the flow. We become blocked; we lose our outlet. We'll only continue in health and radiance if we find a new opportunity to pour out.

Whenever people love, there is a shine to them. The energy passing freely through shows in vibrant expression. When we become tense and strained, restricted, the glow diminishes. We must embrace and care in order to get healed. To become well in ourselves, we must know we still care and it's okay to do so. But how do we do this? We can whisper a message into the breeze and know it goes somewhere, or we can touch a child with tenderness, but we must sprout the new branches of life that show us healthy and living.

I want to be able to remember the happy times of my past. I don't want to put them away in a trunk, afraid to sort through them. If the grief isn't done, every time we think of the trunk in storage, or see a picture and remember, we deny a part of our life. We stifle our loving self and deny the value of the person or the experience in our life. The major reason to work through our grief is so that we can happily view the beauty each experience has brought to the whole. To be able to recall with joy the love given to us or the experience assimilated, makes us greater . . . stronger. We are offered the challenge of life's value system. Can we expand to be greater through this experience?

Do's and Don'ts for Survivors

Have an advisor for your financial and legal problems. Don't think you can do it yourself. Few people can truly function at their best for a minimum of six months; it is more often eighteen months before one functions at his usual level of performance.

Do not change your residence just to create a new environment. There is a lot of basic security in the old pattern even though it is lonely and different. A familiar, daily pattern or life style supports us in our adjustment. Old neighbors and neighborhoods can comfort us and our ineffectiveness is better tolerated here than in new and strange places. Moving in with other family members often starts out with good intentions and high expectations. Rarely does this work out as ideally as it is hoped. It usually is better to do at least a major part of your adjustment before such a move is considered.

As a survivor, while you are making internal adjustments, you are also having to deal with the projections of others. In regular daily communication, people are always trying to clarify themselves to others; explaining, performing, and restating positions, hoping others will know their point of view, their reality. Now, as a survivor, you are faced with the projected fears, frustrations, expectations and old patterns of thinking of all the persons with whom you come in contact. All decisions you discuss openly will have to be seen in the light of others' projections. If you have an advisor, use that person, but know that if you bring up a subject or problem, it is an invitation to the listener to feel that he is being asked to advise you. If you don't want to get another's advice, keep quiet. This will work with some, and at the least, it will slow down the advisors. Whether asked or not, people tend to have a stereotyped picture of the survivor, of how he or she should act, respond, or behave. This is the projection you will have to fight through to find your own rightful pattern.

You need to talk and talk. The support persons who can help most need to be patient and ready to hear the sad story again and again. The new reality is being programmed into the understanding. This period may be longer or shorter according to individuals, but know it is a necessary state, and love, support and listening are major aids at this time.

As you experience loss, it is frightening to find such vulnerability within your own nature. Even the strongest of us will have moments of eggshell fragility and we cannot help but be stunned. Our confidence will come and go. At moments, decision-making comes easy and then the mind seems to sputter, forget, or malfunction. A face and name of many years ago come easily but a neighbor frequently visited produces no name at all. Events of long ago are easily recalled; yesterday eludes us. This is a natural pattern to cope with and to understand as best you can, while you walk through the days of restabilizing. The scattered feelings and ineffective functioning will scare you and tend to create doubt about your capability. Know this behavior pattern is common and do not be overly shaken when it occurs.

CHAPTER EIGHT

Comfort Me as I Try

There are deaths other than physical of which we need to be aware. A perfect example of another kind of death is divorce. Somehow, because the marital experience didn't work out ideally, the whole experience tends to be labeled as unsatisfactory. How common the expression, "I had a bad marriage." Let me share with you another response: A beautiful, live-wire lady I know answers questions about her divorced marital status with, "Successfully completed." How I wish we could all see past relationships as positively.

As with death, divorce presents us the same opportunity for growth, adjustment and failure. Note the similarities. In divorce, the marriage is the patient. Suppose both parties care, do all they can, perhaps get assistance from a counselor (which is like taking the patient to the doctor to get professional help), and try all the prescriptions, but still the marriage dies. We see the couple experience (1) Denial, (2) Anger, (3) Bargaining, (4) Depression, (5) Acceptance. This death process works much the same for individuals, for partnerships, for hopes and dreams, and for other kinds of cycles. Life is created to provoke growth . . . to give us awareness whether we want it or not. How we react, how healthily we spring back, or how much negativity we can release from us, become the vital issues.

Divorce may literally kill people. With hopes crushed, with no reason to live, many people become less and less giving. The giving of self on an individual basis is charging our current of life force. It adds to our sparkle like a diamond being burnished; the light grows brighter. When we are no longer needed or when we are filled with resentment and bitterness, begrudgingly responding to another's prompting, we restrict our free-flowing, natural life force and we diminish. Our lives lose sparkle and lustre . . . we are dying.

If we could satisfactorily complete relationships and move on, loving, caring, not judging nor condemning one another, nor holding resentment, we could be *wiser* from the experience and file it as "Lesson Learned" from the Divine School of Experience.

Can we fully live, on a daily basis, or do we indeed die a bit inside ourselves day by day? In other words, the light which is our life vitality turns on or goes out. Again, the law of life: Change, go forward, or go backward. The vitality of life streams from within us or begins to go out. Light going out is the beginning of death.

The big struggle with this forward movement of life is that we have some problem staying in the Here-and-Now. We tend to drop back into times past and rehash those impossible-to-repeat moments, and often we do this to the point of masochism.

We need to recognize that forgiveness is a part of the challenge of facing life, and thus death. "Why didn't I do so-and-so?" or "If I had only known!" fill the conversation of each one working through guilt, self-punishment, resentment, anger, and loneliness. What we are actually saying is, "I wish I had better savored the experience when I had the chance."

So! Let's get the message! Let's more and more savor the experience of today. This very day is the time we're going to review down the road a bit. Right now, to get the beautiful experience of being here now, alive and alert, lay this book down and go call someone and tell him or her that you care. Share with someone that today your life is better because of the friendship, support, and pleasure the two of you share. Or, write a note expressing your appreciation of someone's impact upon you.

The consciousness of living each day totally makes life worth it. Life very full . . . happily unfolding, makes itself so positive, the pains have compensation. Savoring our food as we eat is a very common idea. Living life day by day is the same approach.

There is a loosely-knit movement called the Praise-to-the-Living Club which suggests we each actively recognize the individuals who contribute in so many ways to our lives. The idea is to take the time, now, today, to write a letter to those people who are adding greatly to one's own life or to the lives of others. Lay this book down and think of those individuals you wish to thank. Encouraging a person now, on a tough day, is much more meaningful than a spray of flowers on his casket later. Writing someone, expressing appreciation for his service, mannerisms, or inspiration, explaining what he has meant to you, make you a member of this worthy Praise-to-the-Living Club. And think of your feelings if you get this kind of boost when you are working diligently with others. What a rich reward!

If we can learn to live up-to-date in this manner, when ends of cycles occur, we won't have such guilt feelings and/or unfinished business with which to deal.

The Be-Here-Now consciousness attempts to retrain us to live one day at a time. "Today is the first day of the rest of your life" implies the same thing. Unless we relate to today as a valuable opportunity to use rather than a time to get through or hoping that tomorrow will change what is unpleasant about today, we will find whole segments of our lives routinely moved through, unappreciated, and, for all practical purposes, unlived.

There is a dreadful saying: "Some people are already dead; they just don't know it." Crude, but oh, so truthful.

The physical body form keeps on, but the spirit, drive, and appreciating consciousness have died from lack of use.

One of the reasons it is so difficult for both professionals and those personally involved to be good support persons, is that it is hard dealing with the pain that gets stirred up. Let's look at it this way. A friendly, sensitive person sees someone suffering—grieving. The kind one steps up and tries to help, if in no other way than just by listening. And what happens? Too often, as the nice person listens, he starts hurting. Remembering a similar situation in his own past, that old hurt comes back and stinging anew, the pain causes him to pull back and lock off his feelings again. Now he's learned it is better not to try to share or even to listen.

A major change of approach offered by new age ideas suggests that people should work through pain and fears rather than swallow them. A counselor filled with pain gets his work distorted by the personal trauma held within. A support person, fearful and distraught, is simply not a support person.

I like the term support person and I use it in its broadest meaning. If I'm your friend and you are suffering, perhaps I can be supportive to you as you cope. I can listen, relieve some responsibilities, do chores, and let you feel my caring. You know I care. You know you have someone to whom you can turn, on whom you can bet. If I'm your friend and if you try to talk to me and I get quiet, withdraw, and even disappear from your life, you are alone. The fact that I could be a friend in a social setting and absent at other times, causes you to feel deserted; you feel guilty for talking about the unpleasant things of life and for letting down the facade that everything is fine. The social code is violated and to get my friendship back means you had better shape up!

Today, a better understanding of human nature is developing. We are now realizing with a more profound awareness that there is something to be gained by a new openness to grief and to the other traumas of life. As some have dared to walk into the pain of others, wading right through it all, they have found themselves transformed. By allowing the pain of another to be mirrored in their own feeling nature, by allowing past hurt to surface and looking straight into it, their own pain has begun to clear. We find ourselves healed by encouraging another who is tired and worn to know a new day can and will come, and by sharing our understanding that life does get better, that hope dawns again in time. We cannot take the grief away, but in our own caring nature, we burn through our old pain, find loving concern, and bring back our own tenderness. As one truly has this experience, he is re-energized. Such sharing, certainly a part of the basis of Alcoholics Anonymous, Parents Without Partners, Parents of Handicapped Children, the Hospice Movement, and groups of women who have had mastectomies, proves the value of the banding together of those who, having tasted the pain, are bound not to let another go through it alone.

Remember, all parties grow. Each of us has lived with skeletons in our closets until, in the support process, we're no longer afraid of exposing ourselves, and when we willingly open the door, we find most of those skeletons dissipate.

A support person may or may not be an involved professional. Most of the time this is not yet a formal title but is found in the hearts and minds of individuals. In time I hope all persons in helping, professional roles will really be support persons.

In relationship to holistic medicine and preventive measures, whether we are grieving persons or support people, Dr. Thomas H. Holmes, a psychiatrist at the University of Washington School of Medicine, devised a rating scale to aid us in recognizing the amount of trauma we are dealing with in our lives. He took a list of everyday experiences and gave each a point value according to its trauma potency. He devised a scoring which indicates the likelihood of developing serious illness. Interestingly, almost all of the major trauma indicators involve the ending of a cycle (remember, this is dealing with a death of some kind). The list follows and as you read it, think of the effort expended in the ending and new beginning cycles. Taking the test can be a kind of "forewarned is forearmed" exercise, and we may then deal with ourselves a bit better as we move through these cycles.

To use the test, circle the number after any event that has occurred in your life in the past year. To find the total amount of stress your family has undergone this year, have each member take the test, add the scores, and divide by the number of members. This average score will reflect your family's chances of developing a serious illness in the next two years. For an individual, a score of 150 or less means the chance of sickness is at most only 37 percent. With a score of more than 300 points, the odds for illness rise to 80 percent, and will continue to rise with the score. Scoring for individuals may be somewhat rough, but if the test is taken by the entire family, the average score will probably be a good indicator of family health. Moreover, individual differences may give warning signs that certain members of the family stand a higher chance of illness than others.

All of these events are natural parts of everyday life experiences and most will affect each of us from time to time. We can learn to guide our lives with some new awareness, for we do have choices about some of these matters; for example, moving our residence or changing jobs. We can be alerted to the fact that we are in an "overload" situation and need to wait before we add to the difficulties. In this way we can help to head off some problems and/or illnesses.

Here is the test, as designed by Dr. Thomas H. Holmes:

SOCIAL READJUSTMENT RATING SCALE[4]

Event	Value
Death of Spouse	100
Divorce	73
Marital separation	65
Jail term	63
Death of close family member	63
Personal injury or illness	53
Marriage	50
Fired from work	47
Marital reconciliation	45
Retirement	45
Change in family member's health	44
Pregnancy	40
Sex difficulties	39
Addition to family	39
Business readjustment	39
Change in financial status	38
Death of close friend	37
Change to different line of work	36
Change in number of marital arguments	35
Mortgage or loan over $10,000	31
Foreclosure of mortgage or loan	30
Change in work responsibilities	29
Son or daughter leaving home	29
Trouble with in-laws	29
Outstanding personal achievement	28
Spouse begins or stops working	26
Starting or finishing school	26
Change in living conditions	25
Revision of personal habits	24
Trouble with boss	23
Change in work hours, conditions	20

Change in residence	20
Change in schools	20
Change in recreational habits	19
Change in church activities	19
Change in social activities	19
Mortgage or loan under $10,000	17
Change in sleeping habits	16
Change in number of family gatherings	15
Vacation	13
Christmas season	12
Minor violation of the law	11

TOTAL

4. Holmes and Rahe, *Journal of Psychosomatic Research,* Vol. ii (1967)

CHAPTER NINE

Insights to Suicide

Many life events are set in motion by factors beyond our control. One of the most painful of these for survivors occurs when someone they love has taken his or her own life. These loving individuals are sincerely grieving for those who have made the conscious choice to end their physical life as they were experiencing it, to opt for something else. I believe this matter may be one of life's most anguish-filled experiences for the victim and for those remaining on the physical side.

To start with, my experience makes me believe that just as life offers a variety of experiences, death or transition does also. However, I have come to believe that most after their physical death, unless terribly disturbed by their act, find a time of sleep or unconsciousness into which to sink or rest for a time.

I've heard the term "twilight zone" used for the plane wherein persons who have committed suicide abide while the balance of their physical plane energy is used up or released so they can truly complete their pulling away from our dimension. With great compassion for those in this area, we must realize they had certainly encountered more pain in their lives than they believed they could handle, else they would not have wished for death. I believe it is this discouragement and the negative attitude of "no-use" that binds the suicide to the sleeping state in that twilight zone.

Two thoughts often expressed need to be discussed here. They are:

(1) If we keep testifying about how pleasant death is and how much easier the next world is compared to this one, we are encouraging suicides, thus leading others into difficulty.

(2) Suicides suffer in the next stage of life equal to their trauma of death. According to the fundamentalist, this time period is forever; according to others, until what would have been the natural time of the individual's physical ending. The second concept generally regards this time period as a kind of purgatory or penance designed by divine law to educate personalities not to violate the gift of life.

Expressed opinions range from quite ugly pictures of suffering and anguish to the sleeping or resting idea of a dull or somewhat subdued plane of waiting.

I am convinced we can send love and prayers to a suicide victim just as to any other deceased person. I suggest these are even more important because this loved one needs a stream of continued love and positive energy to help dissolve the negativity that surrounds him or her, both before and after death.

It is generally believed this netherworld is the overlapping of physical and spiritual existence, a cusp area. The deceased is no longer a part of the physical, material plane with a physical body through which to channel his spirit and yet is not entirely free of the allotted life force given him at his acceptance of incarnation. This concept implies that the spirit entering a body is obligated to experience and do the best it can under all circumstances encountered. To violate this trust is taught as ignorance of divine law, and thus the lesson of respect must be learned.

The purpose of divine law is always to aid one to find the higher nature. We might say God's will is to help us recognize the Oneness of all life. Also, through our process of living, we learn to submit our wills to the higher will. The lesson of living through our periods of trial and darkness to reach the awareness of a new realization is the repeated test life brings. Suicide is the willful act of rejecting life's unfolding pattern and taking matters, figuratively speaking, into one's own hands. I believe most of those guilty of such acts envision a nice, long, peaceful sleep. I feel most persons distraught enough to choose this path are in fact crying out for help, rest, and relief. I also do not feel most are in a regular state of mind, but act out of pain.

I believe that after the act of death occurs, these beings sink into some kind of rest until they begin to stir and again seek experience. If they retain consciousness, even in a faulty or inhibited manner, they will in time move again to know life.

There is a story that Beings of Light and Love move through the twilight zone carrying a bell and a light. They ring the bell and watch for responses from sleeping entities. Anyone who responds to the bell is awakening and then can be helped. Should these beings make an effort to turn their attention to anything outside of their own pain, they will immediately be assisted by the more aware Ones.

Think of this process in the way we know life here in our physical world. Most of us will try to help another if we recognize the need. Those who have the need must give some signal or request to help us know they would welcome our efforts. Once again, it seems we see a pattern of life which demands that one give in order to receive!

Those who rejected life in its physical fullness have to be ready to reach out and again become a part of it all before anyone is allowed to violate their isolation.

I see love and prayers as streams of positive energy we can continue to direct to suicides to help neutralize the painful feelings that drove them to make such a choice. In addition, through the witnessing of the grief they have caused their loved ones, the victims probably incurred additional grief and guilt.

A great effort on our part must be made to forgive the state of ignorance in this area for both the living and for those who have taken their lives. We must consider that the victim acted out of mental, emotional, and/or physical pain and that we weren't able to help much because we didn't realize the intensity of pain or the immediacy of the situation. We, the living, usually are challenged to forgive the suicide for denying us our chance to respond to his need. Also, we have a great need to forgive ourselves for our inadequacy. The great test here is to love unconditionally. To love this precious one, regardless of where and what, becomes the great task.

In all our struggles with relationships, we learn there is a point where we release others to a pattern of their own making. Most of us would choose to protect our loved ones from their hard life lessons. We tell them what to do and what not to do. We threaten, influence, and manipulate to the best of our ability, but often, the willfulness of the individual moves into a pattern of which we do not approve. At this point unconditional love requires release and heart-felt love. The suicide situation truly calls for this letting go and allowing.

Continued grief for years does neither ourself nor our loved one any good. Being a positive, loving person while remembering him in thought and in prayer can be of help. This may be our life challenge now: Can we love enough to refrain from judging either him or ourself as life goes on? Some have suggested that an untimely death is a premature birth into the next world and must have special care as does the premature birth of a baby in our world. I like this idea, and yes, I do believe there is a different experience for those who abort our side of life through their free will. I feel, however, that this is one of life's many lessons through which one learns and grows. Holding this thought, I feel aware ones love, grow, and trust the divine mind to care for all creation in a just manner. I have learned to "trust the word," knowing it makes allowance for those blanks in my understanding. I believe the discouragement, lack of purpose, and limited vision that can cause suicide have to be met and worked through by these precious souls and that a way opens for them to find the resolute strength for this in time. First, these souls need a period of rest, the permission to turn off to it all, until attention is again drawn outward and they can experience other than personality pain. The attachments from personality are strong and outward. The path inward, soulward, is not yet free-flowing or suicide would not have happened. The personality attraction is to look out for assistance, comfort, and even entertainment. Remember the story of the bell, light, or Being that awakens outward interest and thus enables the process of ongoing evaluation to continue. Those more highly evolved spirits, who work as the Beings of Light and Love at this level, bring peace, comfort, and guidance to the one now ready to awaken. They begin the adjustment to a new way of life and the crisis is passed.

Yes, the being has erred in lack of judgment, but we all err. This lesson, probably one of life's most difficult for survivors to handle, requires from us, as we remember, continuing love rather than condemnation. The premature infant requires special handling and this kind of loss also requires special handling and understanding for the survivors.

A good rule to remember is that in spiritual thought, light and awareness are as related as darkness and ignorance. Symbolic language speaks of being cut off from light as painful and of an absence of awareness as being in a place of darkness. Some of this must be taken into consideration in trying to comprehend the meaning of revelation and symbolic scriptures. I believe the divine plan is so all-encompassing that many facets are beyond our comprehension from certain viewpoints. But the understanding we can gain from many experiences leads me to believe no fact is overlooked, and no soul is living out of the sight of the Father-Mother Creator Consciousness.

"I'll lend you for a little time a child of Mine," He said.
"For you to love the while she lives and mourn for when
   she's dead.
It may be six or seven years, or twenty-two or three,
But will you, till I call her back, take care of her for Me?
She'll bring her charms to gladden you and shall her stay
   be brief
You'll have her lovely memories as solace for your grief."

"I cannot promise she will stay since all from earth return,
But there are lessons taught down there I want this child to
   learn.
I've looked the wide world over in My search for teachers
   true,
And from the throngs that crowd life's lanes, I have selected
   you.
Now will you give her all your love, not think the labor
   vain,
Nor hate Me when I come to call to take her back again?"

"I fancied that I heard you say—'Dear Lord, Thy Will Be
   done;'
For all the joy Thy child shall bring, the risk of grief we'll
   run.
We'll shelter her with tenderness, we'll love her while we
   may.
And for the happiness we have known, forever grateful stay.
But, shall the angels call her much sooner than we planned,
We'll brave the bitter grief that comes and try to
   understand."

(Author Unknown)

CHAPTER TEN

Children and Death

There is probably no specific area of death harder for anyone to handle than the death of children. Collectively, we feel the death of a child is more tragic than that of an adult. This has little to do with logic; most say it's because the child has hardly begun his life while an adult is older and more ready for death. In truth, older doesn't mean more ready, and sooner doesn't really mean the breaking of a promise of three score and ten years in which to live out our purpose.

In some part of ourselves, however, we do have a feeling of having been promised children will live to grow up; it is their right. Early death denies that right and righteous indignation surfaces along with the emotions of anger and guilt. Who can one trust if one can't trust God, Life, and the Divine Plan . . . which includes living to be old?

Each year many of us have to wrestle through the maze of pain at a child's dying and try to forgive God, Life, ourselves, and our child for this turn of events. Life turns traitor: First it stimulates us to think of joy, beauty, growing up, potential, and then, having us amply baited, betrays our trust. As parent to the dying child, we feel all this but usually cannot put it into words.

There is also the terrible feeling of failing the child who

dies. The duty of a Responsible Parent is to provide, protect, and guide children safely through the dependent years until this precious trust is strong, capable, independent, and prepared to take life on his own terms. We are heavily programmed from our own childhood that this is the role of parent and most of us try to act it out. We feel guilty over minor accidents, let alone a critical illness during which we may perform heroic feats in order to get the best care possible. Also, the fairy tales prepare us to believe that right wins over wrong, good over bad, and that Life is good and Death is bad. Therefore, the magic equation: If I do this and it's right, plus this and it's right, in the end right wins! Life wins and Death is defeated!

The shocking truth, we sadly learn, is that too often it doesn't work that way. We perform the right acts, we get the right kind of care, we make the demanding sacrifices, we grow, pray, change. But the equation doesn't work. Death can steal the strength and change the robust beauty of a child into a fragile, translucent form. Sometimes Death wins.

Pain and death are synonymous for those involved, but in very different ways. The pain of the onlooker is in many ways more intense than that of the child who is dying. The latter has adjustments to make, but once fear is overcome and the acceptance of poignant goodbyes becomes reality, that one can begin some speculation as to a future life in other dimensions. New expectations and interest often bring this child into a very fine and peaceful perspective. From this encouraging position, the one leaving becomes the one loving and inspiring others.

The onlooker, caught as he is, feels guilty if he wants it over with; feels weak if he cannot control his emotions; feels selfish if he can't bear letting go of the loved one. All of this is magnified if the dying one is your child. You discover you don't wish to get it over with for you'd give your life to hold on for another day. You cannot be weak because you've sworn again and again to be there, to hold back the terrors of the world. You can't cry when you see the child's bravery and have praised him for such spirit.

As the dying one breaks free, the parents stand, as we all do, in the position of trying to stop the rhythm and cycles of life, trying to hold back the movement of the waterfall cascading downward to the earth, or trying with all our might to stop the setting sun. And we cannot.

We look into the face of our loved one and see changes in its hues. We still our personal agony for brief periods of time and, if we dare, bring to the surface unknown courage —or we can run from it all and pretend. Few parents pretend, but many deny.

Parents of dying children go through the five previously outlined stages of death and dying. They are partaking in the little one's death, but in some other place in their nature, there is a second death occurring. It is the death of dreams and hopes for this child.

Usually when an adult dies, a strong part of his potential has been expressed. The individual has lived and acted out choices that have created his life. The crisis of unrealized dreams has been experienced and death, with the maturity of life, has tempered the expectations of all concerned.

With a child, none of this has occurred. We have, then, two simultaneous deaths occurring. One, the real person withdrawing from physical life, and the other, the dreams and potentials that have been energizing our relationship. This second type of death is also experienced by parents of mentally and physically handicapped children.

Be aware that both deaths do not necessarily conclude simultaneously. Frequently the death of hopes and dreams occurs first, especially in the midst of preparatory depression. In this sequence, there is more opportunity for members of the family to experience some peace and tranquility toward the end of the child's life. If the physical death occurs before the releasing of hopes, dreams, and desires, the survivors will have more difficulty in facing life without the child. They are left with no energy to activate new beginnings—"for without my dreams I have no life." This response can be helped by the wise guidance of others who will care and tenderly help the survivor move through the stages to conclude that which had been built.

Those who would help should understand the great warning signs: refusing to talk about the death, and keeping the child's room exactly the way it was to revere his memory. These are indications that the survivor is stuck in a point of pain and no longer is living in the here and now.

Someone has said that when our elders die, we release our past and when our child dies, we feel deprived of our future. I understand what this means: The more one lives through his children, the more traumatic is the loss. If a person is not expressing his own potential and is counting on the child to act out this role, seeing the child as his own extension, the loss is not just of one's child, but also the unexpressed part of self.

There is an organization called The Society of Compassionate Friends, which is now trying to help parents who have lost a child to come to grips with their loss and find new reason for living. The group can be of great help and is anxious to have chapters in areas where as yet it is unknown. If you have such a need or desire to assist those near you in their experience, please write: The Society of Compassionate Friends, P.O. Box 1347, Oak Brook, Ill. 60521 (telephone 312-323-5010).

Parents of physically and mentally handicapped children, as well as those who lose a child, have a serious battle on their hands to hold the rest of the family unit together during the crisis period. The old adage that we "take it out on those we love" is all too true; we cast our feelings of guilt and anger on our mate or other family members, looking for personal relief. If we are not careful, we may find fault with each move others make, damaging the vulnerable, precious bonds of love. Often the depth of our personal pain clouds our vision and understanding; thus we cannot reach a perspective which allows the other persons their own way of coping. As an example, if, from his own pain, a parent pulls back from either the other parent or the suffering child, he is quickly complained about or condemned. Acutely feeling this as a lack of support the parent lashes out causing additional damage.

As people experience this kind of loss, knowing there is no easy way, they need to make the effort to be particularly sensitive to everyone concerned. Everyone involved in the crisis needs to open in an exploratory way, to ask questions, express confusion, and ask for support. Joining a group provides great solace and, in this setting, each parent may observe how others have survived such ordeals.

All that has been said about denial applies here also, for often one of the parents will deny the trauma and thus has to begin to separate himself from the child as time goes on in order to maintain the denial. Remember, the guilt this builds will have to be faced farther down the line. If one fails to reconcile reality and death, or reality and handicap, as we are speaking of it, the great pretense leads one ever farther into a trap.

I had a small son who died, and later, when a second son died a few minutes after birth, I sobbed hysterically. I had four daughters and one son at home and I wanted another son so very much. I felt I could not stand this—it could not be. In my burst of sobs, an older nurse slapped me to reason. She said, "When one chooses to have children, one must know it may go one way, perhaps the other. Grow up!" My tears stopped and I stopped and I stared, dazed through the next few days, finally leaving the hospital with not another tear shed.

In the months that followed, I turned my head when

people neared with babies; I withdrew from the world of young mothers and children. I sent gifts to others having baby showers, saying, "It's too soon yet for me to go." I went through all the outer motions of living and being responsible; I demonstrated I was grown-up.

Later I had another child, a girl. I rejoiced that the child was in good health. All the time I was carrying her, I was afraid to think about the sex of the child. I feared that my selfish wish for a boy had been the cause of death of the son. Perhaps God was teaching me just to appreciate the wholeness of my children and not to be so willful.

In time my family was completed. The net result included a second son, another daughter, plus the two sons living in the next life. Only after I finished having children and in later studies did I finally find a way to cry again. It came through joy, and the door to tears, so blocked by hurt, rejection, and abrupt command, opened.

The love feeling of my death experience became acute and ecstasy was mine. I found joy bubbling through my being and from this place, all things were possible. As I shared, so I received; as I reached out, my cup became filled. My tears flowed once again; first, at joyful times. Then, through forgiving the nurse who had been frightened by my hysterical outburst, I gave up my anger and my long held-back tears emptied.

Since that time, I no longer demand that I always be grown-up. I can laugh again like a child, I can sing and I can play, knowing I can choose to respond in my natural way. That means I also can share my pain with you and you may share with me. I can cry now at your pain, wiping both our tears at the same time, and I know you may smile again, even as I. Love heals. When you suffer so much at the change points in your life, as you grieve, you need some strong support persons to hold the love so you can get well again within its glow.

Pain, in whatever form, has always helped individuals to

come to know themselves better, to find their weaknesses and their strengths. Certainly those blows that strike our children strike us severely, and we are forced to link personal and impersonal love. The great personal love we feel for our helpless child expands into love for all children. We begin to realize in a new way a universal concern for children which can grow into a love for all humanity after our healing process is complete.

Children who are onlookers at another's death have special requirements and there is a most excellent book entitled *The Child and Death* by Edgar N. Jackson to help us assist them to develop a healthy attitude toward death and its part of the life process. The book is filled with wisdom too good to miss, and correlates to the new ways of thinking I suggest. Dr. Robert C. Slater, University of Minnesota, edited Jackson's book and comments:

> Even as we must involve a child in the process of dying and death, it is equally important that we involve the child in post-death activities, not limited to but certainly beginning with the funeral. There are those who seem to possess some unearned wisdom that categorically denies the child involvement in the funeral. As a practicing funeral director, I have seen children of all ages involved in the funeral, and let me assure you categorically that children who are permitted to participate in the funeral will do so at their own level. They usually will show anxiety and reluctance only when such attitudes are conveyed to them by adults. Children are fascinated by the funeral. To them it is the celebration or in essence a party to which many people whom they love very much come, participate and become involved, and they in essence want to be a part of the party.
>
> Dr. Jackson, referred to earlier, has described the funeral as a parade, from the point of death to the point of final disposition. Need I tell anyone how much children love parades?
>
> There are those who would deny the child the value that can be obtained in viewing the dead body and participating

in the funeral and being involved in the family rites and rituals that surround the funeral and post-death activities. I would ask them to consider what sort of impressions and fantasies the child will create if he is denied such participation. If the child is "sent away to be with a friend," what will be the fantasies of that child as to what is happening in the place and with those whom he loved so much who at a time of obvious crisis have denied that child participation therein? We have again but to ask our psychological and psychiatric associates about the problem of dealing with childhood fantasies, especially when they are negative, over against dealing with the child who has been permitted to be involved in actual experiences.

In the process of death education for the child, as far as I am concerned there is no substitute for involvement. I would run the risk of those limited instances in which damage may be done rather than run the much higher calculated risk in which damage would be done if the child is prohibited from participation.

Perhaps it is summed up best by Jackson in a book entitled *The Child and Death* when he says, "When dealing with the unknown, children are often bewildered by the fact that their parents do not know all the answers. Parents, in turn, compound this uncertainty by ignoring their children's questions or by giving long, complex explanations that do not satisfy their children's wishes to know and understand. Children are people with needs, emotions and individual personalities." If we agree with this excellent statement by Jackson, then certainly it is logical to comprehend and to recommend the involvement of the child in post-death activities.[5]

5. Robert C. Slater, "Death From The Beginning," *Thanatos.*

CHAPTER ELEVEN

Pets Are Precious Too

Most of us realize children learn a great deal about life through their pets. Caring for a pet subtly teaches very important information about sex and death and provides an opportunity for learning about unconditional acceptance and love. These subjects are hard to explain, chiefly because of our own pains and confusions. We tend to avoid these subjects until something occurs to provoke questions.

As children, many of us had a beloved pet who died. We shed tears, had a funeral, and later got a new pet. It was highly emotional for us with lots of tears but it may have been much easier for us than for our parents. Often it is. The child's concept of life is relatively simple: yes/no, or, it is/it isn't. The child feels the pain, knowing the pet is gone. Within a short time, he wants a pet again as a friend and companion and knows instinctively the love is worth the price of the pain. As adult sophistication sets in, along with deep awareness of caution, one begins to deliberate these things. The young child needs a pet with which to exchange love just as he needs food to eat, and the child knows this. The adult may choose not to have the pleasure because it is also a responsibility and at times, a burden. These are true differences in perspective.

The child and the pet experience each other as companions, gathering life data together; the child learning responsible action such as having to train the pet. This kind of love isn't restricted to one pet or even one pet at a time. A loving child needs one or more focal points toward which to direct the flow. The pet serves many purposes.

Many of these needs adults have as well, especially the feelings of companionship. Many of us want the unrestricted friendship, the happy greeting, the "someone-loves-and-needs-us feelings" that come with the pet attachment. Most of us know people who have a pet who helps its owners "play" mommy, daddy, and baby. I know a number of such arrangements where people spend a great deal of time and attention on their pets and the pets are as children upon which attention can be centered. In this present time it is interesting to note that more and more young people are choosing not to have children. Often without a child, before they realize it, a pet is chosen and the role is built. I am not implying this is good or bad, rather that it is true, and it will become the lot of every owner some day to lose the beloved pet. And for some, the experience of losing pets is similar to the death of a child. Pets are often surrogate children, whether we realize it or not.

Some people plan ahead and get a younger pet for themselves as the original pet ages, thereby building a bridge for the future so when the elder pet goes, the younger can easily fill the space.

There is often another reaction. Some say, "I'll never love another pet so much. I'll not go through anything like this again. I'm not going to allow myself to get so attached, it's just not worth it."

With these responses, we are acknowledging that every love has a price. The relationship to the pet has high rewards, but it is also an investment of self. I've always felt you have to weigh the energy invested against the reward received. If we have had years of joy, then the pleasure of giving affection, the happiness of romping and moments of tenderness are worth the price of pain.

As a responsible pet owner, each of us is obligated to

many of the responsible parent duties. We are choosing the role and we find ourselves dealing with many of the same feelings. The more the pet becomes a substitute child, the more similar the pain at the time of loss.

Years ago, I had a small, four-pound, precious Chihuahua named Prissy. She was more my pet than the children's. She waited for me to come home from work in a spot just inside the door each day and did special feats just for me. She amazed us all with her open adoration and I got a lot out of the relationship. She was such a tiny, pretty pet and everyone admired her. She was carefully protected—never outside without a leash and the children loved to take turns walking her in the yard.

Two days before Christmas one year, the postal service delivered a package and in the excitement, no one noticed Prissy rush out the door. A few minutes later, a white-faced postman rang the bell saying he had backed over her in the driveway. Brenda, the oldest daughter at home, took charge. She went in my room, got my housecoat, and wrapped Prissy's dead body in it. Amid her own and the other children's tears, she called me at the office. She carefully told me what happened. I put my head down and cried, then decided to go home.

I discovered when I arrived that Brenda and the children had dug a hole in the back yard outside my bedroom window, where she'd be close, and buried her, still in my robe, so she'd feel good. They had all cried; covered the fresh earth with flowers and were making a marker. They talked to me about how they knew it hurt, they told me they didn't want me to see her injured and dead. The oldest child said, "Mother, you couldn't stand it, you loved her too much." They cried; I cried. We all held each other and it really made us very close. I realize now they were responding to innate wisdom and healthy, protecting love. Children, acting out their natural feelings, are usually on target.

Through tears for people, pets, loss and change, we find

some relief. This is a way to let off some of the pressure; we all need this.

In a time when more and more of our society is choosing pets in a big way, we must realize this is a sign of something. It is at least saying pets are important in helping people meet a need, the need to reawaken and express their feelings of love.

Grief, however, is grief, and people sincerely feel grief for pets. There is a real loss and a real hole left in the life when a pet has gone. I think we can safely focus our attention on the goodness that has awakened in us through the responsible action, love, and kindness we have given. Pets do stimulate love in us. Often people who are so hurt that they cannot love a person, will dare to take a pet into their hearts. Emotionally and mentally disturbed children are being helped through pets. Those suspicious, vulnerable persons who avoid others, often can begin to repair through the turning on once again of the love flow through their relationship with an animal.

A key I have found for deep grief over this kind of loss is to count the blessings received from the unconditional love given by the animal friend. The natural question can then arise, "Would you rather not have had this experience?" Following this, I suggest that there is a next stage of life and even if animals do not have souls as we do, they do have spirit and energy, so I believe they go on in a still little understood way. I ask you who grieve thus to whisper a prayer in the wind, bless your pet, and believe goodness is rewarded. You are better for having loved so sincerely and without guard. The life of your pet has made a fine contribution to your life.

CHAPTER TWELVE

My Personal Near-Death Experience

At this point I would like to share with you my near-death experience in 1958. I met what now commonly is called a Light Being. It totally confused me and yet gave me a whole, new sureness about continuity of life. I *know* there is something more. I have experienced part of it.

During the birth of a child I got into difficulty and was given sodium pentothal, a very harmless drug for most people. I had an allergic reaction. My lungs collapsed and my spiritual body separated from the physical and moved to a place of observation near the ceiling. I looked down upon my body and did not know for a moment who it was. Then I realized that it was "me." I watched the hurried efforts of the doctors and nurses. I saw the baby born. I knew it was a little girl. I realized that I was the woman giving birth. Since this was certainly so, what else was happening? I felt like a balloon bobbling near the ceiling. I saw a silvery umbilical cord attaching the "floating me" to the top of the head of the "me" on the operating table. I couldn't understand what was occurring.

Next, I went through a brief moment of fast motion, or whirling, and I found myself out in what seemed to be vast space. There was coolness and beautiful, comfortable peace and stars.

By my side there was a Being with a magnificent presence. I could not see an exact form, but instead, a radiation of light that lit up everything about me and spoke with a voice that held the deepest tenderness one can ever imagine. The voice said, "Look," and I looked into an area that suddenly had a large, golden frame. As I observed, a falling star started in an upper corner and moved slowly, gently across the framed space. As it got to the lower corner, it went out. The voice said, "My child, do not be disturbed. Death makes no difference in the pattern. If you are, you always will be."

At this moment, as this loving yet powerful Being spoke to me, I understood vast meanings, much beyond my ability to explain. I understood life and death, and instantly, any fear I had, ended. There was a totality, a completeness in the realization that I could continue to experience and that there was absolutely no reason to continue my frantic struggle to exist.

For what seemed to be endless time, I experienced this Presence. The Light Being, pure, powerful, all-expansive, was without a form and it could be said that great waves of awareness flowed to me and into my mind.

As I responded to these revelations, I knew them to be so. Of course it didn't matter if one lived or died; it was all so clear. There was a complete trust and greater understanding of what these words meant.

It seemed whole *Truths* revealed themselves to me. Waves of thought . . . ideas greater and purer than I had ever tried to figure out came to me. Thoughts, clear without effort, revealed themselves in total wholeness, although not in logical sequence. I, of course, being in that magnificent Presence, understood it all. I realized that consciousness is life. We will live in and through much, but this consciousness we know that is behind our personality will continue. I knew now that the purpose of life does not depend on me; it has its own purpose. I realized that the flow of it will continue even as I will continue. New serenity entered my being.

As this occurred, an intensity of feeling rushed through

me, as if the light that surrounded that Being was bathing me, penetrating every part of me. As I absorbed the energy, I sensed what I can only describe as bliss. That is such a little word, but the feeling was dynamic, rolling, magnificent, expanding, ecstatic . . . *bliss*. It whirled about me and, entering my chest, flowed through me, and I was immersed in love and awareness for ineffable time.

Then, from that boundless wave I drifted into darkness which flowed over me. At some point, I felt my body being moved and I began to awaken. How could I share this? I tried to talk. The doctor patted my shoulder and said, "Not now, rest." Later, I tried again and again. My experience, beyond any experience of my life, was labeled hallucination. I longed to understand, to find that feeling of love again. Some part of it remained in my heart, however, and that part continues. It is sometimes expanded and sometimes decreased, but it remains a sign to me of another dimension of Love, Life and Power. I think of the feeling as one of Love, although that word lacks its total import. It is certainly much more than that. I have found that when we come together, when we sing and rejoice, when I work with touching and become centered exactly on the person with whom I am working, this flow opens and intense energy rushes through with a love feeling that is beyond expression.

I know it is our nature to examine carefully such experiences. After first being told by my medical doctor this was just an hallucination, I thoroughly accepted his answer. However, when a week later, a similar thing occurred at home, I began to wonder. Several times I had experiences of standing some place apart watching myself sleeping or nursing the baby. I became concerned about these experiences and by the six-week check-up time, I questioned him again. He told me I was under stress and prescribed a tranquilizer. For a period of three to four months I obediently took a pill from time to time and rather forgot the matter, except for an occasional longing to experience that feeling of total love again.

It would be two full years before I would hear a term called "out-of-body" and come to realize the true significance of these "hallucinations."

This experience changed me. My nature became warmer and more outgoing. The sensitivity that had always been so painful was less so, and I could now begin to embrace the world around me more positively. My prayer life held deeper meaning and after those few, unsuccessful attempts to talk to my doctor and others, I kept my secret to myself.

As a child, I had experienced seeing persons who were not present or living and I was left confused. The dying experience and the Light Being now allowed me to feel better about myself. It took some years before a gradual, unfolding awareness led me to know other people, many in fact, who had similar experiences. Presently there are several books available which document the near-death experiences of hundreds of people, indicating that this is assuredly an authentic event.

Dr. Kenneth Ring, a psychology professor at the University of Connecticut, says his studies with individuals who come back from the verge of death suggest five steps to the transition experience. In his work,[6] Dr. Ring concludes: "We do have some form of consciousness after we die."

From in-depth interviews with the survivors, these steps seem to occur:

Step 1: "About 60 percent reported a feeling of tremendous happiness. All bodily pain, sensation, is gone. There are no problems, worries, anxieties, just a tremendous feeling of peacefulness and beauty."

6. Kenneth Ring, *Life at Death: A Scientific Study of Near-Death Experience*

Step 2: "About 40 percent had this experience of feeling either they have no body or are detached from it. It is a separation stage where you become aware that the physical body is one thing and you are something else altogether. It seems perfectly natural, not weird or scary."

Step 3: "For about 20 percent there is a feeling of peaceful floating or drifting through a dark vastness, a tunnel or void. It's as if you are moving but without your body. You are no longer in this physical world but in some kind of darkness."

Step 4: "More than 17 percent suddenly became aware of a brilliant golden light that surrounds them like an envelope of warmth. The light seems to give off feelings of comfort and love.

"People are drawn to it. There is a reluctance to come back out of the light and into the physical world."

Step 5: "About 10 percent have made the switch and are no longer in a transitional passage from this world to what may lie beyond. A person becomes aware of a world of light. Sometimes people will see spirits of deceased loved ones.

"Sometimes they will see beautiful gardens, landscapes, lakes. They feel this place is like a paradise."

This is such a clear condensation of my own experience and has been substantiated so well, that I think we can be comfortable assuming Step 1 brings peace to our transiting loved one. Step 2 finds the body and spirit separation taking place with comfortable consciousness and a natural feeling. Step 3 is the actual floating through the dimensional barrier which usually seems like a tunnel. I believe this is the feeling of floating in water that is often mentioned. Step 4 could be called the meeting of the Light

Being, the Angel, the Love of God or the Life Force. I think our terms should be kept broad because from testimony, the experiences don't seem to depend on religions or spiritual belief systems. Dr. Ring's study summarized this: "So far, then, the work that has been reported suggests that the near-death experience is independent of both religiousness and religious affiliation." Step 5 would be the embracing of those who have gone before, followed by the closing of the door between the worlds. At the last moment, some persons feel a need to return; the others continue into life of a new kind.

Remember Albert Einstein's prediction that we would see the work of the laboratories turned over to the study of God. It's beginning to happen, is it not?

The material of Dr. Ring reinforces the perception that beings greet the one going forward to the new life. His work reveals both the meeting of the Light Being as a common experience for a large percentage of persons, and then later, the meeting of beings that were recognizable to the one having the experience. These beings remind me of the visitation experiences that often occur after death when one catches a glimpse of the deceased in the home or another familiar setting. This experience, although common enough, usually gets pushed aside as fantasy.

Remember, we accept poets when they refer to the spirits and their whispered words; we appreciate artists who paint their pictures of spirits, adding wings. I suggest to you that truth always has been offered to us, but we need to be ready to think about these things before they have meaning.

Be aware, also, that whole religious sects have been based on the possibility of some sort of communication between persons in physical bodies and those in spirit. Modern spiritualism attracts many to pursue these ideas within the context of a denomination of the Christian Church. Spiriualist churches are world-wide with hundreds of thousands of members.

CHAPTER THIRTEEN

Help Flows Through the Planes

Death is not extinguishing
the Light;
It is putting out the lamp
because the dawn has come.
—Rabindranath Tagore

Today, the illuminating works of Dr. Elisabeth Kübler-Ross and Dr. Raymond Moody help many who have had dying experiences. These ideas form a framework of reference for them as it does for doctors and counselors who listen to the stories. We may not understand it all, but we do know it is an experience of many, not the eccentrics or attention-grabbers, but individuals making breakthroughs in awareness.

My search for the understanding of my own near-death experience led me to study mystical writings with new fervor. The message of life after death, of a heaven world, a dimension of many mansions, had new meaning. Angels and messengers became realities to review. Behind each traditional word stood concepts to examine.

I often wonder how many Christians who profess belief in life after death, or continuity of consciousness as it is called in esoteric teachings, genuinely trust their conviction. This is the true test of facing death. For ourselves or for those we love, we have to face whether we really believe or whether we just hope. Hope wears thin in the face of difficult living. Somehow we need to *know*. To me this is one of the most important messages of our current time.

We see doctors searching through thousands of experiences; psychologists, hypnotists, mystics, meditators, all are asking. If you have the experience yourself, you *know*. That's all, you just *know*.

The value of the mystical experience is in the change it produces in the life and reality of the one having the experience. It cannot be given to another. It can be talked about, but the potency of the experience is such that it can never really be completely shared.

It was years later, after my near-death experience, when I had my first spontaneous recall of another life. I remember dying. I will tell you how it feels. . . . Lying here, tired, waiting. I've thought everything through, most of it more than once. I sleep and awake and wait. I used to get frightened by thoughts of death, but not any more. I know I'm ready.

I realize the room is growing cold. I look at my hands and they are a funny color. I've not yet gotten used to this peculiarity even though I've had time. Yes . . . death is cool . . . and death is sleeping and waking. . . . My mind is somehow detached from day-to-day details. It thinks more clearly about things of the past, more about fantasies than matters of today.

Cold . . . then it's pleasantly warm, soft, and peaceful. Silently I find myself moving toward the gossamer Being at the foot of the bed. Glancing back over my shoulder, I see the body lying there. Is it me? Indeed it is, and yet, here I am . . . free and moving without effort toward the kind Presence. Now I know I am dead. Surprisingly, it seems so easy. How glad I am it's done. I feel such a relief . . . effortless, floating, at peace, surrendering into whatever it is that I am.

Always I have struggled to be free; didn't even know what I was struggling for or against. Always active, meeting the next goal, completing my day's work. Dressing, eating, working, thinking . . . now it's done. My book is finished. God, close the cover!

But what is this? I thought it was all over. Now there seems to be more. Where am I? So at peace. Hurrah! It is being done to me, for me. I do not have to try. I relax; I am floating free.

The One who guides me motions and I understand. I think and it is done. No effort, I make absolutely no effort. Pictures flash about me, tears roll down my cheeks. I feel such relief, such comfort. Some memories of the past come and I *know*. Understanding floods my mind. So many thoughts try to crowd into my head, I can't sort them out. I am tired. All of that is far away, so long ago.

I want this peace. I need this rest. I resist thinking back and I want to move on in this effortless, flowing peacefulness. Is this the river that is spoken of? It is a flowing river of life taking me forward, away from the whirling effort— life seems to be the struggle of a piece of driftwood always resisting being drawn into the suction of the whirlpool.

Whirlpool is death and to be avoided at all costs! It ends everything. Then it's all over. I can't go there. I must struggle away from the center or be swallowed up in the nothingness. Run . . . cry . . . scream . . . just don't die!

Now it's done. I move easily, following the Light Form ahead through all the figures, colors, and tones. I have no interest to question or to see. I know that if I want to, I can. The guide is gentle and strong, helpful if I should have need. I am at peace and following freely, relieved of my struggle.

That recollection answered another question for me, the question of reincarnation. Since then, I have recalled several past lives. Each time there is a complete awareness that this is myself in another form. Each time, in retrospect, there are some facets in common with some question or experience by which I am currently challenged.

Several students of mine, making their transitions, have appeared soon after death to let me know of their passing. In psychic or spiritualist circles, it is expected that the beloved will look in on the funeral or memorial service. I have seen discarnate beings at these times trying to comfort family members sobbing in grief.

It is not enough when transition comes just to let go of the loved one. In the past, the Egyptian culture taught prayer for forty-nine days after physical death while the soul moved through a place of review and contemplation. While the Christian tradition does not specify the number of days, it has always taught prayers for the dead and the dying. Likewise, the Judaic tradition has specific customs to help the people at this time. The Rosicrucian tradition suggests there should be a constant vigil, someone praying for thirty-six hours. During these thirty-six hours, the spirit reviews the life experience and is touched by the emotional energy that comes from the earth plane. The spirit's emotional energy is tied yet to the physical family, the loved ones here on the earth plane, and many times beings look back and are aware of the grief of their loved ones. Thus we can understand how we might have visions of recently deceased beings, or see a beloved who has been killed elsewhere . . . sometimes before we physically know of the death.

I have seen several recent magazine articles on the frequencies of people having visions of deceased individuals in the two weeks after death. There are those of us who sincerely believe this is to comfort and help those left behind. Henry Schmales, Jr., Professor of Psychiatry and Medicine, University of Rochester, says, "During the first two weeks after the death and sometimes longer, it is most common for the grieving survivors to have fleeting images of the deceased, while awake or on awakening as well as in dreams." It is also Dr. Schmales' opinion that doctors should tell families about these experiences. "Without this reassurance, the experience can be so frightening to those having it they may think that they are losing their minds.''[7]

I will include here an incredible personal story which confirms that those who pass over continue loving us and try to make us aware of it. When I was fourteen years old, I traveled from Florida to California to visit my father and stepmother and their family. It was to be the last time I was to see him alive, although for years afterward we wrote and shared plans for the day we would get together again. In 1973, after I was a minister and very much involved in spiritual teachings, I was awakened early one morning by a telephone call. I got up and spoke on the telephone with a man who told me that my father had been accidentally killed. My father owned a business that involved heavy equipment and the caller told me that my father had been on a forklift that had hit an ammonia pipeline. In the explosion, he had burned to death. I was overwhelmed; shocked. I hung up the phone and cried. Later, when I was somewhat calmed, I realized I had not asked the usual questions: "When should I come to California?" and "How was my stepmother, Marie?" At this point, I went to the telephone and made a long distance call to Marie. As I began to talk to her, I had a funny feeling she wasn't upset. I asked her about the services and she replied, "What services?" I told her then about the phone call that I had received and she said, "Carol, nothing has happened to your dad. He is right here." As I spoke with my father I thought, "That phone call was the cruelest joke I have ever heard of in my life!" In November of 1975, two and a half years later, another telephone call came. This time a man called my mother, who came to me and told me my father had been killed exactly as had been described in my previous phone call. I called Marie and she asked, "How do you explain this? It happened just as it was told to you."

7. Henry Schmales, Jr., *Emergency Medicine Magazine,* March 1971

For the first time, I realized that I had received a prophetic, psychic "phone call," not a cruel, practical joke. Why? I have decided now it was to give me a chance to go visit; a last appeal, and I did not go. Now that my father really was dead, I had to make the decision about attending the funeral in California. I said to Marie, "I did not come to visit when I could have. I do not want to come now." After I spoke to her, I changed my mind, thinking I would go. But it was impractical, etc., and so I vacillated. Then I had one of the most meaningful experiences of my life as I drove from St. Petersburg to Sarasota one afternoon. On this route there is a very high bridge called the Skyway Bridge. It is spectacular and beautiful, and as I was driving, moving toward the highest point, a presence filled my automobile. I dared not look, but I felt my father, exactly as I had felt him so many years before when we had been together. "Dad?" He answered, "It is all right, Carol, I have come to you." And I said, "I'm sorry I didn't come." He answered, "Understand . . . it is all right. Everything is all right. I understand; I know." I said, "Can I look at you?" and he replied, "Of course." It had been thirty years since I last had seen my dad and turning my head toward him, I could perceive a mist-like presence. He was heavier than when I last saw him thirty years before, with less hair, but I recognized him and felt hot tears of relief and love flowing down my cheeks. I said, "Dad, I love you," and he reassured me, "Don't worry, Carol. I came to you."

We may live in two different worlds, but I believe those worlds overlap at times, especially at birth and death, times of prayer and intense love. Souls moving forward want to and do touch us in some way to affirm that love continues in their consciousness also.

I remember God works in mysterious ways His wonders to perform and that in God's "house there are many mansions." I know there is an eternal life, a life-after-life process, and I am at peace with that knowledge.

As persons who have this consciousness of life-after-life continuity, what can we do to help the one in transition? If we are a friend and aware, yet not as emotional as the immediate family, we can love dearly and impersonally at this time. We need to work from an impersonal, spiritual way in the situation. We will send a radiant, positive energy to the one passing to help neutralize the grief of the family. This is to keep the heaviness of the grief from flowing toward the deceased one.

When we are working with persons making their transition, we should enter into quiet times of meditation, visualization, or prayer, sending a positive stream of love energy to them. If we believe that when we love and care, positive energy is being sent to another, we certainly want to do this to be helpful at this stage of experience.

Ideas that prayers help are applicable here. We send love, light, and comfort to surround the one we are remembering before death, during, and for certain, the first few days afterwards. I usually recommend continuing the practice for at least thirty days.

This stream of positive love energy surrounds our friend and assists this one to respond to those helping from the other levels or planes of existence. When beings move from plane to plane, there is a state of adjustment to be made. The beings, having recently had all their attention focused on the physical life, must now let go and refocus on another plane. For this reason we pray, care, and maintain a stream of non-physical, positive energy around them. This is helpful as the adjustment is made, providing familiar vibrations for them to sustain their efforts.

As I have mentioned, Eastern and Western traditions have all contributed ideas for helping those facing transition, for making the crossing, and for holding the love strong between the planes for a time. A deeper understanding of these traditions provides great comfort for both those crossing and those remaining on the physical side. A new understanding that there is a long tradition of deceased loved ones making themselves visible to their survivors will sustain many as they make an adjustment to their loss.

CHAPTER FOURTEEN

Survivors Face Change

Death, because we see it as so final, intimidates us all. A death touches many people although not all on a conscious level. Be aware a person's death affects his neighbor, the banker, the lady at the local market, the postman, as well as family, friends, and support persons. Because people feel so powerless in a terminal situation, they tend to avoid the individual involved. It becomes too much effort to make small talk or to find a way to show concern and at the same time skirt the emotional issues. When one partner of a couple is dying, the life style of the other one also begins to change. One by one, friends stop dropping in. Eventually, social invitations stop coming because it is felt the healthy mate wouldn't want to attend alone. Of course, some life style change is expected, but not the break in social ties. The changes, including chores to do, trips to town, taking care of tasks formerly handled by the spouse, even sleeping, eating, and visiting, become so difficult to manage alone. Super courage is summoned to do it all. This super courage will be needed for the protection of the dying mate now, and later for the rebalancing of self. When the time comes, the survivor will use this super courage to make the necessary adjustments.

Both need the feeling of having done everything possible, of knowing that family affairs are in right order, and they each need an abundant expression of affection. Both require hope and trust and awareness of the great inventiveness of the Universe.

When a loving tie to a mate is ended, there is the feeling a plug has been pulled out of our life. We have eaten together, slept together, and made decisions with each other's well-being in mind. In fact, the lives were so closely entwined that when one leaves, each life as it has been known, is over. It is equally important to realize that a survivor moves to a new stage of life at this point even as the one making the transition moves to spirit life. A next stage awaits both.

When the death or loss is sudden, shock has the great welcoming value of anesthetizing us to some degree. I call it going on automatic pilot for a time. We do what we have to do. We perform the responsible action and then, when all is done, we begin to feel the pins and needles of our feeling nature coming back to circulation. The pain continues to grow until our logic begins to fail us. We become frightened by our pain, by our periods of not being able to cope, by illogical and emotional actions. Our natural response is to hide.

Hiding our grief, trauma, and fright simply causes the problem to grow out of sight. And grow it does. Eventually it is revealed and we'll burst into tears in public, lash out at some undeserving individual, get drunk and embarrass ourselves, or behave in an obnoxious way causing guilt and regret. As we begin to suspect we're cracking up or falling apart, we may decide to see someone about it and begin the tranquilizer game or hunt for a love affair or postpone it by burying ourselves in more work.

For many people these have been avenues of escape for centuries. They are modes of running away and any and all can lead to greater trauma. I see these as ways to postpone or deny our pain as survivors. Let me say to you that the survivor can no more avoid being touched by the ending of a cycle than can the one dying. If we are in a relationship as friend, parent, or mate, it's two-sided and when change comes, both have to take a deep breath and rebalance. For a brief time other people may share the load, not carrying it nor taking over, but just being there. A crutch isn't wanted forever, but in the crisis, it's needed. A person who has been over the route, knowing how bad it is, can be especially supportive. It's like the young woman who, facing her first delivery, needs to talk to someone who has been through childbirth. It encourages new life to flow and creates the understanding that it can be done.

There is a feeling of a deep hole burned through oneself where the love was, after the loss. This terrible emptiness is, I believe, the worst part of it all. It lives there inside your body in the feeling nature, a constant reminder you are not whole. I have heard this discussed in thousands of words. It is like a hole in the ground when one pulls out a tree that has grown in place for several years. The ground is torn and empty afterwards . . . so are we after our loss, and it takes time and new life to fill in this hole.

It's not a matter of replacing; it's a matter of *new* life. Our experience makes each of us a new person, different . . . even different to the self. So we have to sift through our life, interests, habits, ideas, and philosophy and refine all of them. We have to make room for this experience of change and allow it to make a contribution to the new picture of life we must now carry.

Time helps some, but help comes not from the passing of days but from the new life this time can bring if we let it. I know some bitter, frightened, and angry persons who, refusing life, have not healed although years have passed.

Recently, a beautiful lady with whom I shared my book said, "Tell them to give themselves permission to walk away from the grief at times and come back to it again later." Widowed almost two years ago, she's healing now. She has fought through most of her pain, has days whole and well and then another time of agony appears. She has learned to take life one day at a time and to look her pain in the eye, knowing it isn't just an enemy, but the transmuting energy of life.

Love and pain change us. They help us to reach the most poignant heights of expression. If I know pain, how gentle I'll be as I touch your bruise, for I have suffered so. Searing pain strengthens the Spirit and tenderness is born. Young love is praised for its sweetness, old wine for its seasoned flavor.

Part of freeing ourselves from loneliness comes from realizing that we are alone in life anyway. We can only share bits and pieces of our life regardless of our love. It is wisdom to see that most of life takes place inside one's own head. Our subjective values and perspectives give life its coloring and we all know that two people can witness the same sight, hear the same words, and make two different experiences out of it.

In resisting loneliness, we attach ourselves to the idea of having someone, a particular someone, sharing life with us *always*. We seldom face the fact that while our love is very real and meaningful, each of us spends many hours away from the other, doing something and involved with the life we lead within our own head. Remembering each other with love and respect, we are acting out and gathering experience for our own life, alone. True, some part of this can be communicated later. But the point is, togetherness is more built into attitude, perspective, and imagination than in constant companionship.

Each of us is born alone into this life. We walk for a period of time in touch with many: first parents, then friends, perhaps a mate and children, then more friends. On occasion, we share deeply and meaningfully with different people. But there really isn't anyone in our life who is with us all the time except our own self. This is important to realize because our true security is best vested in the realization that this self is the only companion who is always present.

We may choose to spend part of our time and life with another. Whether it be long or short, we become companions. But it's temporary, regardless of the time period, because we are each on our own track, even if our lives are parallel for a long distance. Realizing this, we can make the time shared with our precious ones even better and we can also accept the responsibility for the need to create some other situation when this time is over.

Part of discovering our true way is to realize we can't make others be "where we are" in understanding, outlook, or experience. As we accept this fact, we begin to enjoy the bonus of having our time together, sharing, loving, and appreciating the goodness of the hour and day, not spoiling it by dread if we see things differently or if we go our separate ways. Thus, we can store up the goodness of life through memories and attitude, using these as building blocks for the future.

The inner self is our one permanent companion and to develop rapport with it is authentic security. If each of us is feeling good about the self, and confident, it helps in the present and may help in the future of this life . . . and, challenging thought, help in future lives!

CHAPTER FIFTEEN

Belief vs. Knowing

The dying experience I shared with you in chapter thirteen was a personal, beautiful past-life remembrance. I was an elderly lady making my transition all alone. I had lived a solitary existence for some years and was unafraid. In fact, I did not want to be disturbed or bothered. Wanting to be with my thoughts in peace, I intuitively knew the presence or reactions of others around me would be disturbing. When I had this recall, I had new feelings about the anxiety felt for elderly loved ones living by themselves. Think about it now . . . wouldn't very private persons and/or those who have chosen to live alone have a different viewpoint from those who regularly need others with them? Our logic tells us that the desired death experience could vary greatly according to the disposition and personality of each individual. In this type of situation, I think the survivor's real problem is that he doesn't want to think he wasn't there when his loved one needed him.

In trying to share with you my personal near-death experience during childbirth in this lifetime, I return to a familiar, old feeling of inadequacy. At the time, in the presence of the dynamic, loving Being, my realization was such that I experienced a clear perception of many things, particularly that life *does* make sense. It *does* have purpose and pattern and I can rest in that truth.

I have spent more than twenty years now trying to find words and ways to share that profound message. As of yet,

I feel I am only scattering crumbs of it as best I can. I approach the task by attempting practical use of these ideas, touching one life at a time, one day at a time.

The vastness of the experience and its revelations astonish me even yet. I have read similar statements from Dr. John Lilly[8] about drug experiences. Repeatedly in poetry, scripture, and in literature of revelatory nature, there is the reference to truth beyond expression. My attempt to express it here is simply that, an attempt.

The question of belief and knowing came up recently on a television interview with Mortimer Adler. He expresses the difference in the two by saying that belief is needed when one doesn't *know*. One can take the logical and rational process to a certain position and then leap by faith to a surmise. Example: belief in after life, eternal life, immortality. You can use all your facts, scriptures, and teachings to help in the structure to get to that belief.

However, when one *knows,* he no longer believes. A person now does not have to leap by faith. No leap is required because of a fact, experience, or reality of which one has possession. One now *knows.*

I have come to the decision, out of love and concern for those traveling ahead of me toward their transition, that I must share my reality of the next stage of life. If we could call on the many who have had experiences that help them *know,* rather than believe, and ask them to share their reality and how they arrived there, we could have a great leap forward in awareness.

Many come to see me to share a personal experience of this nature. Needing to talk about the occurrence, they tell me, "I've never shared this with anyone, or anyone outside my family." If we weren't so quick to condemn that which we do not understand, persons could be encouraged to share experiences helpful to one preparing for death.

8. John Lilly, *The Center of the Cyclone*

Mortimer Adler, ardent student of Aristotle, the Greek philosopher, shows how, in the refined thinking process, individuals come to a comprehension of continuity of consciousness and a realization of the prime mover of life. Adler, a Jew, is one of the leading authorities of the teachings of Thomas Aquinas, great father of Christianity. Asked why, since he understood Christianity and its teachings so well, he never had joined its communion, he replied he had not yet found the "resolute will to walk in the path of Jesus Christ." His family is Episcopalian; he has been responsible for many accepting the intellectual side of Catholicism; he readily states he believes in God.

I think this is an example of enlightened thought bringing an awareness so broad and encompassing that one leaps over the divisions and lines of religions to the realization of the whole: God. Aristotle (not held accountable for being non-Christian since he lived before Jesus!) found his Truth through philosophy. A Jew, M. Adler, pondering those Greek ideas while also exposed to the finest of Catholic thought, leapt to the realization of the oneness of life. All minds fed and stimulated through philosophy, beauty, and refined logic become open to the power, rhythm, and flow of life. Open-ended lives begin to make sense if we free ourselves from time and space limitations. This means the mind can go beyond the body even now.

The next step, when we dare, is to think a new way, listen to new thoughts, stretch to a new dimension, and if we can get a process of openness started, we can free ourselves from biases, programming, and the limits we have allowed to restrict us. Interesting that a belief in a "prime mover" can help one appreciate Greek, Jewish and Catholic thought. Could it mean the oneness of life can truly be realized?

In any period of search and change, one must go through some degree of experimentation to find techniques and concepts that work and are acceptable for helping deal with the business of life and the challenges it offers. Today, many are exploring new ideas and ancient ideas for their contribution to the quality of modern life. While discrimination must be used in this as in all matters, there is much of life too exciting and wonderful to miss should we be unwilling to take time to explore and evaluate. Blind and automatic acceptance of others' ideas is ignorance. We all are trained and taught many things, especially as children, that need to be re-examined as we mature into thinking adults. We may choose to continue just as we were. That's fine, we have made the choice. If we never look, however, we may wear old and useless ideas, habits, and concepts to clothe a new and great life. Think of it, if we still gave the same value to a dollar that we did in our youth, we'd be hard hit today. Some of us are still in that rut with our understanding of change and growth. At some point we all need to think a new way about things just to see the view from there!

In a business management seminar I attended once, it was suggested that we sit on a high stool instead of regular office chairs for one day to see how different our work area seemed to us. Being creatures of habit, we regularly put up with inefficiency and unnecessary inconvenience once we are used to something, failing to notice how it hinders us. To give new ideas opportunity to grow, we must listen, evaluate, and play with them, asking, "What if . . . ?" I see this as a mental, stretching exercise. Gradually, as we come to find the hints and experiences of many people which substantiate some of these new and different ideas, we become more comfortable in exploring concepts anew.

Torkom Saraydarian, a new age philosopher and teacher, offers suggestions and techniques for living up-to-date.[9] I have adopted many of these and use them with students

9. Torkom Saraydarian, *The Science of Becoming Oneself.*

and clients. One of these is particularly appropriate to our use to prepare for the transition period. It is as follows.

In a quiet and meditative mood, as detached as possible, begin to visualize the death we await. As we create our death, let's make it as pleasant and comfortable as possible with all the people present that we desire. Put in other aspects as they suit you, for as we write the script, we can do it our own way. For example, if you are now terminally ill, you have some facts to work with; if you are not, you don't. So begin to create the ending of this stage of life and prepare for the beginning of the new.

Now visualize yourself in the coffin, family members reacting to the news of your death, friends helpful and tearful. Be conscious of business matters that would fall upon others, perhaps property and possessions that would have to be disposed of. What else does your particular life ending leave "up in the air"? As you get strong resistance to these thoughts, know this is perfectly natural. Most of us resist doing such thinking because it is unpleasant and it is a lot of work. In this relaxed and detached awareness, be open to thoughts of your inner nature. Do you need to give some kind word to another? Do you need to forgive another or release another from a debt? Who really cares for you that you fail to recognize? Would you like to leave something to a particular person that you haven't thought about before?

See the wisdom in such forethought? I hope you do. I know a number of individuals who are trying to think in such a manner so that they can leave others well aware of their love and memory in a happy, comforting kind of way.

It is important in this kind of exercise to make notes afterward and to act upon some of the impressions you get. This stimulates the inner nature to remind you of other affairs to put in order, and other people who love and care about you who need a remembrance. One lady I know made out Christmas cards to some number of her friends including a "last" note. She wanted to say she cared one more time and this was the way she did it, leaving the cards to be mailed the following Christmas.

Do not think this is an exercise just for those who are informed about a terminal illness. It is equally meaningful to everyone for the awareness it brings of the hole left in the lives of others when you withdraw. Think of a drill corps with one dropping out and the adjustment required by the rest to close ranks. We all touch more lives than we know. Sudden death is very much like this, but any major change does much the same. Just think of the loneliness often brought on when a family, near and dear, moves to another residence or city. Change hurts. By making an effort such as this exercise, we are becoming more aware of our interlocking ties and we will always honor them with new respect as a result. We can dedicate ourselves to being more in touch and up-to-date from here to the future.

CHAPTER SIXTEEN

The Power of Touch

Recently I worked with a gentleman who suffered amyotrophic lateral sclerosis, more commonly called Lou Gehrig Syndrome or ALS. This slowly, advancing condition brings death through deteriorating muscles as gradually, the patient loses all movement. The physical body refuses any activation from the consciousness within; the personality is, in fact, the prisoner of the body.

This is one of the clearest examples we have of the difference between the body and consciousness. Also, I feel this can help us see that the thinking, indwelling spirit is truly not the body, but the user of the body.

In this extreme, diseased condition, the mind of the person is lucid, intelligent, functioning, while the body is unusable and is dying. The prisoner within awaits the point of death as a captive, knowing that in time the breath ends, vital functions fail . . . and the body loses its hold on the spirit. I think this is an obvious demonstration that our spirit and body are merely working together for a time.

In our lifetime, most of us will have the opportunity to observe someone whose mind is very clear as his body is dying; or the reverse, we will see perfect physical bodies with the mental faculty gone. These illustrations help us realize that our physical, emotional, mental, or spiritual natures may fail to cooperate. From this we perceive more clearly that life, especially constructive life, depends on a balance of these components.

I think of my friend who had ALS, and of his struggle as a consciousness with his body a cocoon about him. The death of the body ended its grip on the spirit within. The consciousness escaped the body and began its life in spirit.

I had a dream one night about a year ago. It came to me long after I had been counseling in this field and I felt I had worked through my own fears of death. I had had the death experience of which I have written and was quite content within myself in this regard, or so I thought.

In the dream, a teacher I love and respect came to me and showed me a symbol, saying that when this sign occurs, I'd know I was dying. The particular sign came to pass and I recognized it. I, having complete trust in the teacher, accepted the validity of the sign and acknowledged death to be evident.

I awakened frozen stiff, realized it was a dream, and lay there evaluating the situation. My breathing was rapid, my body was rigid, my heart was pounding. I got out of bed, thinking about the dream. I thought about my life— was this a warning? I really thought about what was most important to me at this particular time. Finally I went back to bed.

Since then I have given consideration to this dream a number of times. I believe that our dreams come to us from our basic, subconscious nature, and that all of us are connected through a collective unconscious. We call it humanity, or the human qualities we share. The physical body is of this humanness. It is our vehicle of expression on the physical dimension and it is, in fact, terminal. The body does die and the fears of dying belong to the body and the physical part of our nature. The spirit, the soul, the next-dimensional inhabitor of the body, knowing that it continues to exist, does not carry the fear. As we know ourselves best in the physical state, we are more in touch with the outer, physical nature of ourselves than the inner essence, so we express the body's trauma. In one sense, we might say we instinctively know the fear because we know the body. In the same way, we know the need for food, sex, comfort, security.

If we can know the essence of our inner self as well as we know the external self, we are getting somewhere. We begin to recognize what part dies, what part doesn't. I think of a beautiful automobile and our attachment to it while it is new; but as years pass, we gradually appreciate it more for its usefulness. As the natural sequence of events will unfold, we'll again get excited, happy, and proud of another vehicle. The soul, in its wisdom, knows the body is needed, appreciates and uses it, but knows it serves a function. The body can be realized as a functioning part; the spirit can be realized as a separate intelligence. This is the greatest value of "out-of-body" experiences or the "near-death" experience. They reveal to an individual that there is a true ability to function separately. I think the lesson is to fully realize that we are not a body with a spirit, but instead, a spirit with a body. Knowing this, we, the spirit, can drop the body and find our immortality; also, we will recognize the mortality of the body without becoming defeated.

As people reach this level of understanding, they will be in a position to share with others. A remark often heard today is "I'd like to help but I don't know how." There is the recognition that dying ones need intelligent, loving support. This is why books such as this are being written, lectures given, and so many ideas and suggestions are being made. If there is a hospice or death and dying counselor in your area, call and ask questions. I've recently been told that there are roughly fifty hospices in operation now. I know there are several spiritual groups and churches with death and dying discussion formats. In addition, colleges and universities can help you contact similar groups in your area. This book gives the new vision: You *can* do it. The key is feeling the inner desire to help the next person in the way that you recognize you need someone; become that kind of friend. This means a willingness to share the hurt so no one else feels the rejection and loneliness you have felt, or that you have seen in the lives of others. It means a willingness to share new perceptions about the indwelling spirit and the body vehicle.

A suggestion I have, if you will be such a support person to someone who has been told he is dying, or even if he just suspects it, is to use a lot of touching. Just as an infant can be reached through the subconscious and made secure by rocking or holding, so can adults. Taking walks, holding hands, sitting close; remember, as much touching as possible! Usually sexual needs are erratic and undependable and easily misinterpreted, so put the attention on just being there within reach, and wait for the timing which signals it's time to talk. There is no formula except to be natural. Statements like, "I really don't know either, but I'll be here," "We'll ask about that," and "I care and we'll manage," become strong building blocks. They are truths, not flowery promises, and this openness and honesty is felt and gives comfort. This is equally as true with children as with adults. The aware, support person looks straight into the eyes of the suffering one and says, "I care. I'm here, let me help. I don't have to do anything, nor do you; I'll sit here. I can stand to hear you cry. I'll hold you in my arms or dry your tears. I've felt it, too."

In the supporting role, just as touch is a major comfort for one approaching death, massage, a form of touch, can be of primary aid to the survivor.

Massage has been an especial help in cases of sudden death or suicide. In the anguish of the situation, it is almost impossible for the bereaved to relax. Almost always the first hours of shock are so unacceptable, the survivor agonizes to the extent that sleep is impossible. Only in rare situations should medication be given.

While these hours are extremely difficult, coming to terms with death in our own way is critical at this point.

Much therapeutic help is often required later if this period is blocked. Supportive friends need to be a part of these hours and there is little one can do except care and listen. The grief has to come out or great damage will be done. We need some ideas to guide us in this area.

Some time ago, I found that giving a massage works wonders. The touching, caressing of the physical body does help relax the nerves some, but much more important is the sense of security achieved by the touching. We all need to be held, rocked, caressed, and told in no uncertain language that others care.

Massage is a way that works if we, ourselves, can be comfortable with this much touching. I have found a technique that seems to be a healing touch. One does not need much professional skill to give a helpful massage. To develop confidence, I recommend a massage workshop. Get the bereaved person you are working with to strip to underclothing and put him or her to bed covered with a top sheet.

Start with the shoulders, arms, and hands. Use some lotion or if not available, simple vegetable oil from the kitchen. Gradually work out the tension of the muscles of one side, then the other. I touch and care, and I do little or no talking. Nearly always, the patient will cry and talk to you. This is excellent. The talking is therapeutic. An occasional, "yes," "Is that so?" or another non-judgmental comment keeps the stream of release flowing. After both sides of the body and legs are done, I ask the person to turn over and work heavily on the back, which is the area where we carry responsibility, and then down the back of the legs.

All of this is done slowly and repeatedly. The goal is not to get finished, but to keep the patient releasing his grief as much and as long as possible. It is not unusual for me to spend one to one-and-a half hours here. By the time this is done, a great deal has been accomplished.

Finishing, gently massage the face. Tenderly and quietly

you conclude the treatment. In some psychological way you are now rebuilding; getting this one ready to face the world again.

Even if a person can't sleep now, you have been intimately involved with him during a most traumatic period and you've stayed with him supportively. He is well aware of your caring and this is desperately needed in shock situations.

When one copes with the shock of sudden rejection, such as a loved one disappearing deliberately or committing suicide, the massage is invaluable. These experiences leave such indelible scars on the psyche that as support persons, we want to render whatever immediate first-aid we can.

The bitter rejection experience often causes individuals to feel sexually inadequate and emotionally insecure for years to come. It is not uncommon for this type of experience to lead the survivor to pursue one lover after another, trying to deny the rejection and prove acceptability. We are in a unique place if we can be of immediate service and prevent some of this damage.

Similarly, the suicide of a loved one chills the heart so badly, one freezes with fear. Never knowing when love will be withdrawn again, one becomes afraid to love and blocks the very flowing force that could heal the life. An attitude of "I'll never place myself in such a vulnerable position again!" is quite common. These lonely persons lead dead lives, guilt-ridden, fearful of each day, berating themselves for their own immature, past actions or even for the actions of others. Therefore, compassionate support is one of the most loving gifts we can give to one who suffers in this way. Find your technique, a way to openly express your caring so that you, too, may be a positive life force giver!

CHAPTER SEVENTEEN

Useful Techniques for Today

Many ancient, sacrificial customs, trips to the temple, rituals and tokens are seen as foolish today. I suggest that those rituals were of greater value than we realize. They helped less sophisticated people show love and appreciation, gave directions for showing grief, and provided a means for releasing the intense emotions surrounding a loss. In our new, modern, less traditional attitude, we must rebuild some of these tools that are needed for the releasing process. Rituals will work for us when we believe them; the faith we place in a technique gives it its potency. Rituals help us cope when our intellect is cutting in and out, as they do under the shock and strain of grief-filled times. The dynamics of the spiritual services of all faiths are designed to aid both those who have passed and those left behind.

Part of the present difficulty with traditional vs. non-traditional views is that as some people are awakened to new concepts, they assume the old ways to be valueless. Since they have not yet constructed the next ritual or pattern to help in times of trauma, they are frustrated.

One contemporary approach being tried is meditation, a process of contacting the inner life. I describe it as touching in with our true source. Whether or not we know anything about spiritual life, this process happens to us spontaneously through daydreaming at a deep level as we actually lose contact with the outer world. This touching in, often called meditation, has a comforting, restoring effect. We forget our cares, float free of daily life, and get many of the benefits similar to sleep from these recurring relief periods.

When one learns meditation for psychological reasons, certain benefits occur. Biofeedback can monitor the psychological changes as they manifest at the physical level. The psyche also experiences something but these more subtle changes cannot be so easily demonstrated.

Both Old and New Testaments of the Bible support ideas of "entering into the silence of the Lord." Eastern teaching, suggesting more inner work than outer display, provides many techniques we can incorporate. The mystical Jewish Kabbala and esoteric Christianity, using Christian Mystery School patterns, encourage meditation as one of the four major spiritual disciplines for all disciples. The other three disciplines are contemplation, prayer, and adoration.

Meditation is touching into the God Force within, or as may be more commonly expressed, contacting the Holy Spirit. This silent, inner experience is to strengthen one and to increase the spiritual power or force in the life so one becomes fortified by the Living Presence. In new spiritual verbiage, it's touching the stream of life itself.

While there are many meditative approaches taught,[10] the most helpful in regard to death is the idea of following the light within. Light, symbolic of inspiration, wisdom, and intelligence, becomes the symbol of the Life Presence without form. This picturing of light filling the mind, head, and then body is magnifying the oneness with the flow of life. It is taught that we can attach our consciousness to the stream. Flooding our being with light, surrendering to it, becomes a way to flow with life, while in a physical body and afterwards. By the ritual of focusing upon the presence of light in meditation, one begins the process of shifting

10. Carol W. Parrish, *Meditation Plus*

from outer to inner worlds. Therefore, today many people are learning to meditate in preparation for the death transition as they move from the physical to spiritual worlds.

An expression repeatedly used in all spiritual teachings in regard to meditation is to "follow the light." Many visualize a white light to represent the formless God of the Universe, the Creative Source. Others find their minds fill with an inner light as they reach a deep, inner contact point. All traditions use some form of the word, light, to represent the guiding presence of God. With our contemporary insight into this tradition, we have a new discovery which is called the Light Being: a novel idea, yet undoubtedly the very basic experience of countless numbers before us.

The great reason one is taught to follow the light or go to the light at death is for safe passage through the astral dimension or assistance in transitting the emotional plane. If you've never heard these words before they can sound foreboding, but the ideas can be comforting and a bit of knowledge about this can be helpful.

A part of the physical world consists of a less dense, less solid dimension sometimes described as a shadow of the physical plane. This level overlaps the physical and accounts for the appearance of loved ones after death, and even the accounts of ghosts that we hear of from time to time.

It is taught that this plane is made up of those transitting people more in touch with the dense, physical world than with the spirit level and those not wanting to move on for whatever reason. Often, for example, a young mother might lag behind to look after her child. An older mate might wait here for a partner of many years. A great many human traits affect us for some time after the immediate passing of the physical body. This is especially so if we have great emotional concern or unfinished business on earth.

Several ancient traditions had extensive literature for this process; probably the best known are *The Egyptian Book of the Dead* and *The Tibetan Book of the Dead*. The two are considerably alike; they are difficult and of little help without esoteric understanding. However, if properly studied, they serve to acquaint us with other cultures which had more understanding for we find great similarities between the near-death experiences today and the ancient writings. As more share and experiment with meditation and inner work, the meaning of the material becomes clearer and many of the ideas are comprehended.

There is an exercise that is recommended to those who wish to grow spiritually as they understand more and more of the wisdom passed to us from the ancient Truths. It is called the daily review and in this practice you set aside a few minutes each evening and think back about the entire day.

You review the events of the day *backwards,* allowing each event or experience to be weighed on its own merits. When events are reviewed chronologically, they tend to run together, with the emotion of each incident pouring into the next as they do in the sequence of life. By going over them backward, one must divide the events into segments, breaking that sequence, thus requiring each occurrence to stand on its own merit. This causes one to recognize the energy or focus which started the event, your own contribution to the build-up of positive or negative energy, and your response.

When you find a situation in which you wish you had responded differently, there is additional action that can be taken:

(1) You can think how you wish you had handled the situation. For example, wishing you had responded lovingly instead of with hostility to unkind remarks. You can, in fact, in mind and with mind, recreate the situation and act out in the mind a changed sequence of responses: See yourself keeping calm, staying centered, and responding gently,

quietly, or even lovingly. This retake of the situation, while done inwardly, is actually helping to re-program, helping us learn to respond in a manner of our own choosing.

It's much like practicing your part in a play until you know the lines perfectly. In the reveiw you are able to hold your emotional nature clear, to respond lovingly, and without explosion, you allow a triggering point to pass. The name of the game is to deal with the incident to your satisfaction. You gradually learn to conquer disturbing actions and the underlying emotions as well.

(2) In addition, if we believe thoughts are things and if we can damage one another by hate-charged emotion or anger we loose or direct to another, we can spiritually attempt to make amends through this exercise. In the review, since we are now calm and working from the spiritual level of ourself, we can attempt to balance the destructive actions. In a loving way we can send forth thoughts of forgiveness, we can appreciate that other soul and its particular struggle, and we can send a stream of loving energy from us, accepting responsibility for our actions and our responses triggered by the hostility of others. We really begin to *be* the loving one. Spiritual students seeking to live a divine life get much assistance from this exercise. It requires daily thought about how we each respond to life and its experience. If we release, justifying our responses, we can begin to be what we want to be.

This daily review is of great value when we begin to think of dying and the life review. Stories of life reviews are told by many who experience near-death or death experiences. Reference is often made to near-drowning experiences when "My whole life flashed before me." Dr. George Ritchie's experience, described in *Learning To Die*, [11] is certainly an example. There are also biblical references to a judgment day after or in conjunction with death. In the esoteric tra-

11. Jon Mundy, *Learning To Die*

dition the belief is held that the Christ Within views the life and judges it and helps the personality to learn from its experience. Thus, students in the daily review seek to correct and upgrade their everyday life by continually trying to review their experiences from a spiritual level. In this manner it is possible to balance from the life level rather than from a spirit level after death. It is believed this pattern speeds up the evolution of the soul, awakens spiritual qualities within, and produces a more spiritual personality, thus realizing the goal of a disciple of divine life.

I would like to apprise you here of another new level pattern which may become a ritual, a spiritual tradition, in our time. This concept to which I refer is the inception of crying rooms in hospitals. This includes a psychotherapy approach of mourning, crying, screaming, and grieving openly which is a process rapidly building favor in the eyes of those in direct contact with the bereaved. To allow one to get it all out as soon as possible sets such healing into motion that it is one of the blessings of our new approach. Since sex can now be acknowledged, perhaps death can be looked upon as equally natural.

A young psychologist involved in Death Awareness Counseling in the Cincinnati area told me that if she lost a close friend or a family member, she would immediately enter a death group therapy class or go for private counseling, another modern approach which is becoming more and more acceptable. In her opinion, this is today's best way of getting through the re-balancing process so one can again pick up the business of living. I support this idea in theory but I want our society to adopt an approach which goes a step further.

We should not place the burden upon an individual to seek out such aid, but we should create a holistic approach to death. I envision a process of interlocking lives so that dying is done at home with the family. Hospitals and nursing homes are needed and well serve some situations, but even here we could find ways to humanize the situation. Much change and creativity must occur for these urine-saturated, drugged atmospheres to be converted to loving places within which anyone might want to live or die. A new breed of caring people is awakening to these sensitive situations and through the discontent being stirred up and the new ideas being inspired, I expect much change.

One change which is new to the American scene is the hospice. Eagerly accepted by most, the hospice concept is designed for the care of the terminally ill. The foremost goal is to help the patient remain at home until death among their familiar setting and loved ones. In some areas the hospice actually has a facility purposely constructed to create an informal place for patients to be well cared for while encouraging pets, children and friends to share this time. The hospice idea suggests one be allowed his last desires as much as possible. A great deal of effort is made to prepare each person in the family as well as close friends for the end of life by helping each one live positively day by day and hour by hour.

Hospices, new to most of us, are introducing natural methods of love and caring to the fearful experience of death. While professionals are appreciated and sought to become part of each hospice, there is a great realization that there's more to death than the clinical aspect. A strong interest in the whole family participating makes for an atmosphere of support and integrates death into the wholeness of life.

Volunteers are sought and trained to work with doctors, nurses, social workers and spiritual counselors. Volunteers are accepted from every walk of life. A sincere desire to help is as important as any credential. Persons having experienced loss usually are of the greatest benefit to others facing the experience. Each day is allowed to unfold without a hospital atmosphere. In most cities, as of yet, the movement consists of an office, some trained and dedicated professionals, and a large number of loving and helpful adventurous people.

The strength of the movement has grown from the generosity of the dedicated workers. The hospice idea is meeting a need in the lives of the patients, yes, but equally so in our society. A new way of facing death is being sought. I expect us to see many variations of these in the immediate future.

For additional ideas write or call: National Hospice Organization, 1311-A Dolly Madison Blvd., MacLean, Virginia 22101, (703) 356-6770.

As you can well surmise from these remarks, I am totally in support of the hospice movement. I believe in addition, from a practical point of view, that much of the high cost of medical care can thus be circumvented. If we begin now to become involved in the whole process of care and death, we can put life into a better prospect for our own future.

Individuals who may be involved with the patient professionally and/or personally are all support persons. We automatically think of friends and family, but we must extend that picture to include the professionals giving attention and advice. Also, professionals must be helped to know it is expected and acceptable for them to give some sincere caring from their personal selves. Otherwise, we might as well cease referring to this group as the "caring profession." This list certainly includes doctors and nurses, but also includes attorneys, bankers, ministers, priests, and rabbis, social workers, physical therapists, and emergency assistants. Last, but by no means least, we must include funeral home directors and crematory specialists who have needed skills. There are others, according to the specific situation. All these occupations have grown out of the human need. In becoming capable, professionals often become cool and detached. Most of the cool detachment is self-protection, a way of not really getting involved for a person who may have no real answer.

Believe me, there *is* a real answer: Share the experience! Speak of it honestly, admit you can do little but care, but do your caring openly. Let the patient hear you say, "I am sharing your experience. I am here." In this framework, he gets permission to be totally honest, to be real. There is the freedom to think out loud, cry, ask someone to sit awhile and tarry with him this day. If professionals can be intimately connected to the situation, the family members, friends, and even the patient, all get a model for the roles needed to develop a real support system, even if there is no monumental solution. Our nature is such that we do mimic one another. We follow the pattern of those we admire, and at this time in our society, professionals are highly respected. As support persons, professional and personal, the new call then is to *care* as we share, freely, honestly, and openly.

CHAPTER EIGHTEEN

Traditions on Review

We can hardly explore these many aspects of the closing stages of life, the question of continuing life and assistance for principal and survivor, without moving naturally into the subject of funerals and memorial services.

At a point when social traditions are rapidly changing, some feel compelled to follow the custom of religion or family tradition. Others, repelled by rituals or customs which seem sterile or uncaring, cry out for a new way to deal with such a tender time.

I think it is important to remember all that we have previously said about style as we try to find the way that will work best for us. People have their own styles, their own personal mannerisms. I remember crude remarks made about fashionable funeral masses for Mafia members some years ago. Many have stereotyped pictures of persons, wealthy and supposedly unethical, receiving a most Christian burial; the life style and service seemingly are in opposition. Similar to this, political and business persons believed to be unethical, are eulogized in glowing terms when they are gone. For these and other reasons, much of society is reaching a point of resisting traditional funeral arrangements. Today, the public is reaching for some answers that can meet more appropriately an up-to-date code.

We are realizing that to be consistent and true, the funeral must suit the person just as does his clothing or his home.

Because the home is more or less a good reflection of the individual, I often support a memorial service in this setting.

If a person is a regular temple or church goer, yes, his service probably will be most fitting there. That worship participation has been vital to the life and the ritual will be an appropriate salutation of the life. However, if the deceased has not been actively engaged in religious worship, has not participated in years or perhaps was never inclined that way, why not recognize the life for what it did value?

New approaches can be and are developed to replace outgrown or unused ritual. One of the most natural, comfortable, and sincere is the home memorial service. At this time, more and more people are breaking with tradition in order to have a service of deep, personal meaning for themselves.

The home memorial is a gathering of close friends and family to celebrate the life of the deceased. Each service differs, but an air of informality is the rule. A minister may speak and/or guide the service, with close friends and members of the family taking part. Often there is a reading of some of the thoughts of the deceased or original or favorite poetry is selected. Children may read a poem, sing a song, or express their thoughts. This is a time for a loving bon voyage for the departed. There may or may not be food afterward. More and more there is an emphasis placed upon picking up the pieces and going forward, recognizing the good that has come to each life through its contact with the departed person. Pictures are often displayed and the idea of contribution and rejoicing for blessings received is emphasized. There is a definite feeling established of closing one door and opening the next. Thus, the human need for helpful ritual at changing points is fulfilled. Often, as I see these healing, loving times, I think of the passage in Ecclesiastes declaring the day of death being better than the day of one's birth. Only now are we beginning to deal with the wisdom these words contain.

Memorial services must be arranged sensitively, according to the family and situation. It is to be as personal as you care to make it according to the tender feelings of the group involved. Avoid detachment, formality, and triteness. The idea is to build a safe place of deep love to help in healing the grief of those left behind. This healing force comforts and encourages new life to flow and while it is the sendoff for the deceased, it is also a major turning point for survivors. The healing force aids them to let go of the past and begin to think of the changes ahead. These services are needed to help us have a feeling of completeness and of turning a corner to the next segment of life. We do not need to do away with the tradition of funerals and memorial services; we need to learn to use them in a more constructive way.

These rituals are indeed painful because they remind us so much of our own vulnerability. Intellectually, we all know our days are numbered, but we do not wish to be reminded. When one close to us disappears behind that veil, we react from a deep and vulnerable place within our nature. The more natural life and death, or the idea of life and continuing life becomes to us, the less trauma we will encounter. The less we experience this kind of trauma, the more naturally we respond to others in their varying situations and the better support person we become.

Suppose you are not ready for such a home memorial service yet. Consider an informal church service. It's harder to be informal in that setting, but certain things can be done. Several friends can speak and if the music is changed, and the words "celebration of life" are used, some barriers naturally come down. Family attitude is the major factor. Greeting friends warmly rather than withdrawing indicates a new understanding of the situation. In this setting, reading favorite poems, perhaps original pieces by the deceased or the family, is really effective. Speaking of the person in a close and personal way with a sincere manner rather than the euphemistic eulogies of the past makes the difference. Clothing needs to be less formal, brighter, more natural.

Sometimes an informal gathering can be held in a park, at a lovely beach or in the yard or garden, if such is possible. Think of this, especially for one who loved nature. Do not feel you are locked into any arrangement. You are expressing your love and appreciation for this one's personal contribution to your life and structuring a setting in which others may feel your love and express theirs.

Your style is your particular way of expressing a nature which is unique to you. My style is the manner I use in writing this book, my personal insights and reactions to life, the combination that has the stamp of "Carol" on it for me. Your style rings true for you. My words represent me; yours carry your personal resonance of truth. Everyone is made up of his or her own special realities, arrived at in his or her own experience. That combination of realities, mannerisms, energies, and insights is clothed in the way you think, dress, talk, and react to events. Your approach to pain and confusion, joy and happiness, new people and events, change and death should reflect your unique personality. Sometimes a shock sweeps you out of your style for a bit, but as you re-balance, individuality should return. If we don't like something about our particular style, we have to eliminate a quality, a fault, or an approach through the cultivation of something more preferable.

Energy moves, cuts little rivulets in the brain called patterns or habits. These patterns, once embedded, are not easily changed, but they can be altered by effort or modification of the patterns. Since the style of each person is made up of the accumulation of a life's perspective, change usually comes slowly and only with patience and hard work.

In the news in recent months has been a special story of a man's family who gathered around him in his last hours, sang all his favorite songs and played guitar music, sharing his final time in this way. Because this man was famous, it made the news, but many such experiences are occurring throughout the world.

The hospice concept suggests one be allowed his last desires as much as possible. Elisabeth Kübler-Ross tells of deaths which have included wine and candle light. Children can be held tenderly or pets curled up at the foot of the bed.

Some of these ideas seem strange when we first hear of them; they are so new. But which would we choose: to be drugged out of consciousness in a hospital or to be free of drugs or only slightly medicated (an advantage of a hospice), and if at all possible, to have every last moment together?

Realize also that these new ideas make life much more guilt-free for families. They can participate in the life of the loved one to the last, especially in a home atmosphere and relaxed setting rather than in a strange corridor or limited visiting plan which especially exclude beloved children and pets.

I have encouraged home care whenever possible, with family and friends participating in the real life drama of death. We all need to be part of Life and Death, even to be prepared for our own turn. I suggest singing to the dying one, or reading and writing poetry. Never mind that he or she cannot respond. The spirit is conscious and knows and wants you near. Read letters from friends, tell the news of others and *touch*.

Several times I've advised gentle, ever so gentle, washing or massage with lotion over the body in the last hours. If there is no pain at touch, this is most comforting. Even if the person cannot respond, if you know there isn't pain, gently rub or stroke with lotion. Stroke, hum, sing, visit, play the favorite tunes. Write letters to others and read them aloud . . . ever mindful that you're being a best friend, a support person all the way.

If you are questioning the degree of medication the patient should have to keep comfortable, inquire through your physician or the local hospice about the Brampton mixture. Quoting Elisabeth Kübler-Ross, "With the help of G. Humma, a pharmacist at the Indianapolis Methodist Hospital, a handbook of the Brampton mixture was developed and became available to any physician who was willing to try this marvelous cocktail and who was encouraged to send patients home to die without the need for injections and frequent medical supervision."

I don't believe this book would be complete without a reference to a document commonly called *The Living Will*. This type of request is growing in popularity and anyone can prepare such a document, have it witnessed and added to his or her legal papers. It certainly serves to help professionals and family know the strong feelings of the signer. Such a decision is extremely hard for a family to come to in the midst of a crisis. Often any talk of taking a person off a support system invokes great guilt in parties involved, even when one has had strong, logical arguments previously.

Following is an example of a Living Will:

TO MY FAMILY, PHYSICIAN, LAWYER, CLERGYMAN
TO ANY MEDICAL FACILITY IN WHOSE CARE I HAPPEN TO BE
TO ANY INDIVIDUAL WHO MAY BECOME RESPONSIBLE FOR
    MY HEALTH, WELFARE OR AFFAIRS

Death is as much a reality as birth, growth, maturity and old age—it is the one certainty of life. If the time comes when I, _____ can no longer take part in decisions for my own future, let this statement stand as an expression of my wishes, while I am still of sound mind.

If the situation should arise in which there is no reasonable expectation of my recovery from physical or mental disability, I request that I be allowed to die and not be kept alive by artificial means or "heroic measures." I do not fear death itself as much as the indignities of deterioration, dependence and hopeless pain. I therefore ask that medication be mercifully administered to me to alleviate suffering even though this may hasten the moment of death.

This request is made after careful consideration. I hope you who care for me will feel morally bound to follow its mandate. I recognize that this appears to place a heavy responsibility upon you, but it is with the intention of relieving you of such responsiblity and of placing it upon myself in accordance with my strong convictions, that this statement is made.

Signed _____

Date _____

Witness _____

Witness _____

Copies of this request have been given to _____

_____

_____

For additional information, write Euthanasia Educational Council, 250 West 57th Street, New York, NY 10019.

Yes, it's a courageous time of change that we live in. Often, when we think of the fear in life, we fail to realize that much is being done to raise its quality. Dying at home, surrounded by your loved ones and pets, with someone reading you poetry or singing your favorite songs in the light of candles or with the sunshine streaming through your own window, certainly has a lot going for it. Let's try it!

Do not overlook the idea that tradition still plays an important role in many people's lives. If it has been helpful and important to some in the past, it will help now. Be aware of what is meaningful both to you and to the taste of the deceased. To be of help, many who plan ahead talk about their own memorial service, discussing and planning with mates or family. This is, of course, the very best way. It takes a safe, loving, support system for a dying person to openly discuss such plans. Don't expect everyone to be able to do it.

Burial or cremation should be discussed as it gets terribly difficult in the time after the death. If an individual feels strongly one way or the other, it should be known and respected. If it matters little, be sensitive to the mate and then the children. Be gentle in exploring ideas together for each idea may be wrought with fear. As the discussion progresses, emotion is everywhere. Each one should be gentle and sensitive, knowing this to be delicate work, touching subconscious ideas, fears, memories, and bringing the long, unfaced pains forward, now to be dealt with.

By virtue of their profession, ministers have had to deal with such matters as these, but it does not mean they deal with them well. Often they are most guilty of professionalism that is permeated by their personal denial to face their own suppressed feelings. The death and dying counselor is the one most prepared to be of help here. He has usually faced his own pain and has dared to be vulnerable or he wouldn't be in this particular field.

Individuals who staff funeral homes and/or crematories are in a unique situation. Their role can become one of manipulation thriving on emotionalism and pain, or one of the greatest kind of service. The opportunity to serve those in pain, grief, and often shock, is unique and can be a high, ethical service. Not everyone in these professions can rise to the desired level of performance, of course. There certainly is, in our society at this time, a need for workers of great sensitivity with the awareness of a need for change. Since these workers can be great support persons for the survivors of any death situation, it is important that they be inspired and dedicated individuals.

Aware persons, supportive and loving, will examine these suggestions for a newer approach to funerals and memorial services. Let us hope that, matched to unique life patterns, they will be incorporated into a meaningful modern tradition.

CHAPTER NINETEEN

Life and Living Includes Death

The challenge of our time is not to debate right or wrong, traditional vs. non-traditional. It is to accept death, inevitable for all of us, as a part of life, then incorporate it and its preparatory stages into living. We begin by playing with new and varying ideas, and as we can, use them as we deal with the occasions presented to us. For many at this time, just talking openly about the subject is a big step forward. There is a great relief when that happens and the dying one and the survivor can openly discuss that which presses closely upon the mind and heart of each.

It's difficult to understand how Christian ministers could speak out against such works as Dr. Raymond Moody's *Life After Life*. To date, this work encompasses the newest scientific efforts possible to report a recurring experience that points to an afterworld, and every Christian minister has been saying this in some manner since the words came from Jesus' lips. Another powerful scientific investigation of near-death experiences is a new book (1980) *Life at Death* by Kenneth Ring. He seeks to look in an objective manner at the experiences of afterlife.

What is it that keeps Christians from standing in one accord, celebrating this great step in research? My feeling is that this resulted because there is no clear-cut heaven/hell issue in the book. If half the revived or resuscitated individuals had come back describing the pain of hell-fire and the other half had come back exclaiming over harps and music, many ministers would have rejoiced, for this has been the traditional message. As it is, because there is no misgiving in the information we've gotten from these revived people, the fear of God isn't evident nor are people inclined to seek out the Church to help them "change their ways." For this reason, the evidence seems contrary to those preaching eternal life. Maybe more than ever the loving beings encountered by so many are trying to show us God is much more loving than we are; I certainly hope so.

As we work with dying individuals, we find there are many new ways to handle unfinished business. I think of a most proper, loving father who held much anger in his heart regarding a daughter who had not lived up to his expectations. She was living with a young man, they were not married, and he considered this a great sin. He had disinherited her, he wouldn't allow her name to be spoken in his presence, and he dealt with the matter as if she no longer existed.

In his last days, I brought this up, making reference to unfinished business. He didn't want to discuss it, feeling totally justified in his stand. I told him I was terribly sorry for his daughter and was shocked at his cruelty. I called to his attention that he was, in fact, condemning her to live with his disapproval the rest of her life. As long as she lived, she would remember him with feelings of condemnation and separation. All her memories of the loving father of her childhood would be overlayed with his disapproval. If and when she changed life styles, begged forgiveness, suffered, whatever it was he would have for her, how could he then let her know she was forgiven? Because I believed he would be continuing on, I suggested that perhaps he could find a way to let her know, but also asked him to consider the possibility that he couldn't or that she couldn't accept forgiveness sent in a gentle way from spirit. Could he not say to her now, "I love you, even though I do not approve of your actions?"

Before his death a few weeks later, he called his daughter on the telephone. Though he couldn't change his mind about his disapproval of her life style, he told her he loved her. By the time he died, he and his daughter were assured of the continuance of their loving relationship.

We all need to ask ourselves if we should carry our hostility and condemnation for others to our end. Or should this be the time, as we contemplate with new awareness the biblical words, "forgive us our debts, as we forgive our debtors," that we let go of earthly matters, loving and forgiving, so that we can go on about the business of spiritual growth and allow those we forgive to continue to grow and change according to the spiritual self within them.

Death must be faced whether a person is spiritually inclined or not. Perhaps ministers can help spiritual people according to their own denominations; this has been the supposition. However, when Dr. Kübler-Ross challenges groups, including ministers, to say that they really do believe in a next stage of life, few accept the challenge.

My sharing is meant to be just that, a sharing of experiences that serve as material for individuals to think about. I *know* a form of life continues and this I would share to give comfort and new hope to many who do not know.

I feel life continues and not in the clear-cut heaven/hell, Judeo-Christian concepts. I believe that in the Father's house there are many mansions and we know very little about them.

I think the whole history of art, drama, inspired thought, and mythology offers us ideas about angels and a spirit world. The biblical references are certainly frequent; the Hindus make reference to the devas; the Hebrews have the Netherland and its inhabitants; the ancient Egyptians had Tuat, the common name for the abode of the departed, and throughout time individuals have told their ghost stories. Phenomena, however frightening at times, intrigue and attract us because we do not comprehend the hows and whys of another dimension. I think these clues to Truth are hidden in the most obvious places, in everyday life, waiting for our need or our desire to find it.

If we can still sense the spirit of ancient Egypt in the King Tut exhibit or feel the power of an absent artist in his work, why can't we believe in the spirit of an individual continuing?

I am convinced that that which has been set into motion by the great creative Source of life continues. The law of physics states that energy only changes form; it cannot be destroyed.

I believe, emphatically, in life here and there, onward and upward, linking together a chain of humanity, our lives and souls intertwined. Whether we know or hope or care, humanity moves forward, made in the image and likeness of the intelligence of the All.

We come to *know* death as a friend.

LET THERE BE PEACE

Epilogue

obituaries

Mary Parrish Rotunno, 22, in Pasco vehicle accident

By SHARON KIRBY
Clearwater Times Staff Writer

CLEARWATER — Mary Parrish Rotunno, 22 of 612 Seabreeze Drive, Port Richey, died Tuesday (Aug. 19, 1980) when a pickup truck driven by her husband flipped into a canal in New Port Richey.

Born in Clearwater, she was a life-long resident of the area. She was a Clearwater Central Catholic High School graduate and a member of Our Lady of Lourdes Catholic Church in Dunedin.

Survivors include her husband John A., Port Richey; a daughter Alexis Marie; her mother Mrs. Carol Parrish, Sarasota; her father J. Scott Parrish III, Pinellas Park; two brothers, William N. Griffin of Bradenton and Mark J. Parrish of Hudson; five sisters, Brenda Dulje of Hudson, Susan Aubertin and Judy G. Parrish, both of Pinellas Park, Karen Parrish of Sarasota and Patricia Griffin Cassidy of Portland, Ore.

The family will receive visitors from 3 to 5 p.m. and 7 to 9 p.m. Thursday. A service will be at 10 a.m. Friday at Our Lady of Lourdes. Burial will be in Parklawn Memory Gardens, Palm Harbor. Moss Dunedin Chapel is in charge of arrangements.

128

Times DIGEST

Girl, 2, dies after accident

Two-year-old Alexis Rotunno died Thursday as the result of a truck accident Tuesday in which her mother, Mary Parrish Rotunno, 22, died. Her father, Alexander Rotunno, 30, driver of the pickup truck that flipped into a canal in Gulf Harbors, Pasco County, was treated and released at Community Hospital. The child, who lived with her parents at 612 Sea Breeze Dr., New Port Richey, was reportedly trapped in the vehicle in five feet of water for nearly 20 minutes.

If I had to write this book today, I couldn't. This week I buried my twenty-two-year-old daughter and her two-year-old child. Mary Beth and Alexis lost their lives in a one-car automobile accident. Alexis was asleep with her head in her father's lap as he drove the family home late in the evening. The day had been good; he and Mary had enjoyed themselves.

The peculiar chain of events began when Alexis awakened and pulled herself up, using the steering wheel. The unexpected pull flipped the truck sideways just as the vehicle crossed a narrow and unrailed bridge. The fashionable Florida subdivision had dug channels to create water-front lots. The channel beneath them was twelve feet deep.

Twenty minutes later, Mary Beth's body was pulled from the water. It is believed the blow to the right side of her head had knocked her unconscious; she was pronounced dead on arrival at the Community Hospital. The paramedics worked feverishly to resuscitate the baby pulled from the vehicle. Her heart started. After being rushed to the small, local hospital for emergency assistance, she was transferred by ambulance to Pediatrics Intensive Care at Tampa General Hospital for the finest care possible. Sixty hours later, she joined her mother in death. Realizing she was severely brain-damaged, we watched the beautiful body complete its effort to survive and came to understand, from personal experience, the struggle of wanting life to continue yet aware of the healing that death often brings.

On Friday, Mary Beth and Alexis were laid to rest together. My heart is touched by the love and gentleness of many persons. Again, I had seen first hand the drama of death. Coming home, I picked up the manuscript of this book to reread it and to see if my words, echoing back to me, could stand the test of my experience. I find the words ring true and I have added supplemental insights. I offer them to you.

Touching the body, hair or hand helps us to deal with the reality and finality of the physical life. Just as long ago families dealt with life and death close up—births at home, self-doctoring of wounds, and washing and dressing the bodies of their own deceased, we are again beginning to participate in these previously unmentionable experiences. Participation in the total life experience makes us holistically well beings.

More and more we are realizing we need to be fully conscious, undrugged, facing birth, with its joy and its pain, with our love flowing. By embracing our bodies, our method of bonding lives and families together is called forward. Strengthening our ties to one another at these crisis points helps us to be responsible participants. The multidimentional levels of each one of us have opportunity both to grow and to bond. If we allow as many crises as possible to be handled by professionals and outsiders, how do we find our true strength? In our avoidance of the pain, we usually miss one of life's most poignant moments. We need, as a people, to stop thinking someone else knows what to do better than we, ourselves. The professional can, of course, be a support person, but personal integrity, strength of character and stability are found through rising to the painful occasion life has presented to us.

One of the most painful experiences of my encounters with death came when preparing for the funeral of my daughter. The task of selecting the casket and clothing was mine. The time came for selecting a shroud and there was no way I could let my fashion-conscious, lovely, young woman wear the old lady frocks on display. Most of her clothes were sunback or modern sleeveless, and I simply couldn't go home to her closet and get something. I found myself in a mall shopping for a suitable outfit. Engaging that strength we all have, I "gritted my teeth" and just did it. I looked until I found a cowl-necked, cotton sweater like the ones I had given her for her last Christmas, and a lacy jumper she could have worn and enjoyed. It mattered a lot that she wore what was natural to Mary Beth.

To walk through the mall, a natural part of everyday, twentieth century life, and select clothing for your dearly beloved deceased is a test of endurance. Only a heart brave, but also loving, can do this. As I looked at her wearing the garments later, I thought how pleased I felt. I had participated in preparing her in this way. I helped my levels of self integrate the past and the present, and also found strength to help build my future.

I now struggle with the loss of my daughter and granddaughter. We call such happenings tragic accidents, yet there is a place in me that knows these events are part of the fabric of life. I am comforted in my loss, made certain by the knowledge of that time with my own encounter with death, that gentle Being of Light we know by such a fearful name. I hold tightly to my own death experience as my conscious mind struggles to compute the reality of this new loss into my everyday life.

As the author of this book, I need to acknowledge how I find myself reacting to this occurrence. It amazed me to observe parts of myself dealing with the reality of this pain-filled event. I believe my struggle to integrate and comprehend the experience is the struggle every one of us shares. This is part of our oneness.

At times my head is in silent, unruffled, smooth peace. My mind computes, calculates, plans, realizes all the many details I must take care of. I think about gas for the car; messages to be telephoned to others; etc. Then, at times, even while the smooth flow of thought is in the foreground of my mind, I feel the stirring of a new wave of pain growing from another level. This pain advances upon me until it breaks my conscious line of thought and the rational mind loses its grasp for a brief respite—the wave of grief is followed by a second or two of relief—no thought—then memory re-invades and either tears flow or a deep breath restores the thinking process.

I believe this is the natural pattern of grief and repair. I feel the process happening within myself and capture it to study. The emotional nature feels like a deep ocean, the surface being the mental part of myself. When I'm observing, I know I am driving my car, answering questions, or making arrangements for flowers. Then, even as I am conscious of the sun shining or of the surface activity, another grieving part begins to feel the stirring, the working to the surface from the depths. The rolling wave has begun. From the slightest recall or recognition, word, or prompting, the motion begins to grow. I resist knowing the pain is on its way as long as I can, denying the surge coming to the foreground, not wanting to deal with it. It's like standing at the beach watching the waves come in. Useless to run

screaming at the water . . . "Stop! Stop! I've had enough!"
Useless to fight the pain, for the waves are a part of life—
not mine, nor yours, this pain belongs to Life.

This pain is Life's. So the mind stops and allows the wave
to invade it as the dry beach sand accepts the water of the
sea wetting its surface. The wisdom of the sand knows the
tide will subside. This kind of grief subsides, not because
one no longer cares or eventually learns to cope, but because the expansion of consciousness occurs to help us truly
know both living and dying are part of the natural process.

Look at the seashore: The water and the sand are naturally
working, creating, and expressing together.

Dealing with my personal grief makes me acutely aware
of the levels of myself which are interacting. How many of
us are watching that process on any given day? There is the
wise level, the philosophical part of our nature, that says,
"Well, I believe so-and-so," or, "I *do* believe," or, "I
know it." This part does know and is trying to support the
actions of the other levels.

Another part doesn't know anything and doesn't even
want to. This part just hurts. It doesn't care what the doctors say, or what the reasons or explanations are. This part
needs to cry, to scream, to hit something! It bellows its
scream of agony skyward.

Black and white they are. Then there is the integration of
the two, all the multitudinous shades of gray. The flash of
insights, the incidents of recall, the happy memory of last
Christmas, the sense of relief, "I'm so glad I did such and
such," and the feelings of regret over the undone or unsaid,
are weaving themselves together into one pattern. The
pattern we shape, or at least help to shape, forms our
character. We respond from previously developed habit
patterns, spiritual strengths, expressive routes and energy
levels of our being.

We may find ourselves out of bed, walking the floor,
because the energy level has gotten too high or tense. If we

can release some of it, we can then go back to bed and perhaps to sleep.

People will also get up and unconsciously slip into habits of smoking, drinking coffee, saying the Rosary, or some similar, religious ritual, cleaning out the cabinets, perhaps taking a walk around the block. These motions can all be done from the rote part of self. This is using an old performance to stabilize because it KNOWS how to function, but not yet how to change within the perimeter of these sudden, necessary adjustments.

Gradually the new pattern is learned. As I try to think of my world without Mary Beth and the baby, I am acutely aware of the hole blown in the fabric of my existence; aware of the abrupt rupturing of my picture of her future and of my part interwoven into that future. Hopes explode in midair; plans jettison without my consent.

The wise level of self puts in a word or two, interjects great wisdom which my mother/grandmother personality doesn't want to hear. Mother/grandmother wants to say, "I can protect them. I deny this—I won't have it! Turn back the frames and let's replay this part of the movie. I demand a different script. This can't be so!"

The wise and knowing part, vastly in tune with Life, brings its wisdom to mother/grandmother and says, "This is the stuff character is made of. You are a child of the Universe and you will experience what the Universe has to offer!"

Once life is conceived, its entire rhythm is to be experienced. Breathe deeply; learn to flow with it. The great pain of your labor will be followed by the incredible beauty and joy of new life.

The age-old wisdom comes to us from every direction. A day ends; a new one dawns. Yesterday I buried my daughter and grandchild. Happily, today a man tells me of the birth of a new child and I smile at him with love. He has thus assured me of the continuity of life. Yes, it is